Mansion Fare

Mansion Fare
The Culinary Heritage of Oklahoma's Governors

Rhonda Walters
First Lady of Oklahoma

Photography by David Fitzgerald
and
Jim Argo

❖ Graphic Arts Center Publishing™

International Standard Book Number 1-55868-150-7
Library of Congress Number 93-78577
© MCMXCIII by Graphic Arts Center Publishing Company
P.O. Box 10306 • Portland, Oregon 97210
No part of this book may be reproduced by any means
without the permission of the publisher.
President • Charles M. Hopkins
Editor-in-Chief • Douglas Pfeiffer
Managing Editor • Jean Andrews
Editor • Nancy W. Shearman
Designer • Leslie E. Holcomb
Production Manager • Richard L. Owsiany
Color Separations • Agency Litho
Printer • Dynagraphics, Inc.
Bindery • Lincoln & Allen
Printed in the United States of America

foreword

The Governor and Mrs. David Walters in the Mansion dining room.

To me, food is much more than mere sustenance. Rather, it's a lifelong interest that meaningfully expresses the unbroken traditions of life on the Oklahoma prairie — hospitality, care for others, and family unity.

That joy has continued over the years as I've grown from schoolgirl to young bride to mother of a growing family to career woman to First Lady. Food — and the warmth, togetherness, and love it so often signifies — has always been a focal point for David, the children, and me. We've never lived in a house where we didn't remodel the kitchen, and, of course, the best parties with friends and family always end up in the kitchen. In so many ways, it's the center of our world.

We've maintained these traditions since moving into the Governor's Mansion. Whether an elegant state dinner, a casual pool party, a down-home breakfast, or a quick bite on the run, food pulls us together, conveys our mutual affection, and soothes our souls. It's a value shared by families across Oklahoma.

With this book, I offer you a personal glimpse into a meaningful part of our lives and the heritage of this wonderful house Oklahomans allow us to call home. It's a privilege, indeed. Many of the fondest times for the Mansion's occupants have revolved around the grace, style, flavors, and scents that have historically flowed from this kitchen.

I hope you will try these recipes in your own kitchen and savor them as we and other First Families have done. I trust these recipes, which form a memorable part of this home's heritage, will find a welcome home with your family, too.

Rhonda Walters
First Lady of Oklahoma

contents

The newly constructed Oklahoma Governor's Mansion in 1928.

the mansion

The Oklahoma Governor's Mansion's public and private rooms, completely redecorated with private donations in early 1991 by Mrs. Rhonda Walters, exude the quiet elegance of the English countryside. Rich colors, textures, and patterns provide a visual tapestry for all who enter its doors. Over the years, the Mansion has undergone several renovations, yet it continues to retain its historic integrity.

Personal mementos, photographs, and the sight and sounds of children are found throughout this elegant home, proof that the Mansion is a private home as well as a public institution.

The first floor, traditionally considered the Mansion's public area, contains the entry foyer with grand staircase, formal living room, library, dining room, governor's study, sun room, and kitchen. In these rooms, the Governor and First Lady host visiting dignitaries and friends. The most recent project involved renovation of the kitchen and private living quarters to meet the needs of a large family with children.

The Mansion library in 1991.

The first family's living quarters, four bedrooms, an office/family room, and a sun deck, are located on the second floor. A ballroom and a small kitchen occupy the third floor.

Governor Henry Simpson Johnson and his family celebrated Christmas 1928 in the Mansion's library.

In 1927, the Eleventh Oklahoma Legislature voted to provide funds to build the state's first Governor's Mansion. The appropriation provided $100,000 — $75,000 for the structure and $25,000 for furnishings. As Governor Lee Cruce suggested in 1914, the Mansion would be located in the prairie field two blocks east of the State Capitol in northeast Oklahoma City.

The architectural firm chosen to design the Mansion was Layton, Hicks, and Forsyth, a regionally famous team from Oklahoma City which had designed the Capitol and other significant structures throughout the state. The only instruction to the architects was that the Mansion design should complement the Capitol. With this in mind, the designers chose to face the exterior with the same type of limestone.

The Governor's Mansion in 1928 from the east wing of the State Capitol.

Their plans specified a modified Dutch Colonial design with a Spanish-style red-tiled roof. Simmer Construction Company of Oklahoma City was awarded the project. Construction began during the summer of 1927, and was completed in the fall of 1928. In October 1928, the Mansion was officially dedicated and Governor Henry Johnson and his family became the first occupants.

Originally, the Mansion included 19 rooms. Located in the basement were a storage room, a laundry, and heating boiler. Air conditioning was not installed. The first floor contained a grand central hall which led to a distinctive circular paneled staircase. Off the hall of the first floor were the library, sun room, living room, dining room, breakfast room, and kitchen. All of these rooms, except the kitchen and breakfast nook, had ornamental plaster ceilings, walls paneled in walnut, and built-in cabinets with leaded glass.

On the second floor were the Governor's office and five bedrooms, three of which had ornamental plaster ceilings. On the third floor, the grand ballroom, complete with a fine maple floor and a fireplace, offered a final touch of elegance.

Initially, landscaping was delayed due to insufficient funds, but in 1929 the Legislature provided another $39,000 for the construction of a matching garage, servant's quarters, and an ornamental iron grill fence with limestone pillars. Trees were planted and gardens were placed, as well.

Since those early days of 1928 and 1929, every Governor has lived in the comfortable home, positioning the Mansion as a hub of politics and government in the state. The Mansion is open to the public each Wednesday, except holidays, from 1 to 3 p.m. Tour its interior and stroll the grounds rich in Oklahoma history.

Mansion Formal Dining Room, 1991.

Mansion Formal Dining Room, 1928.

The Mansion's foyer where guests are greeted upon arrival, 1991.

The Mansion's Governors

1928 - 1929	Henry S. Johnson
1929 - 1931	William J. Holloway
1931 - 1935	"Alfalfa Bill" Murray
1935 - 1939	E.W. Marland
1939 - 1943	Leon C. Phillips
1943 - 1947	Robert S. Kerr
1947 - 1951	Roy Turner
1951 - 1955	Johnston Murray
1955 - 1959	Raymond Gary
1959 - 1963	J. Howard Edmondson
1963 - 1967	Henry Bellmon
1967 - 1971	Dewey Bartlett
1971 - 1975	David Hall
1975 - 1979	David Boren
1979 - 1987	George Nigh
1987 - 1991	Henry Bellmon
1991 -	David Walters

Family quarters on the second floor of the Mansion, 1991.

The kitchen, formerly consisting of a butler's pantry and main kitchen, was completely remodeled in 1991 by Mrs. Walters to accommodate seating of their family and to improve traffic flow. The counter tops are Oklahoma granite. Two windows were uncovered in the renovation.

The South Lawn of the Mansion is frequently used for outdoor entertaining from formal dinners under a tent to barbecues.

breakfast

Donna Nigh, wife of former Governor George Nigh, in office from 1979 to 1987, recalled this breakfast:

A breakfast was held each Monday morning during the session for the leadership of the House and Senate to work out their legislative programs with the Governor. It became a challenge to prepare different menus each week for the same twenty people. This particular week we had prepared French toast — no easy assignment to have it come off at the same time.

Just as we prepared to serve, they got into an argument in the dining room and all the legislators walked out — refusing to work with each other. One of my all-time memories is of George standing in the driveway begging them to come back in and eat because "Donna made French toast." He must have known how angry I was going to be. In retrospect, we should have served that soggy left-over toast the next week.

Senator Rodger Randle arrived at the Mansion as George and the angry legislators were leaving. Oblivious to the disagreement, the Senator entered the dining room, fixed himself a plate, and remembers to this day that delightful breakfast of French toast.

The early morning habits of Governors Bellmon and Walters are very simple.

Governor Henry Bellmon, who served from 1963 to 1967 and again from 1987 to 1991, was an extremely early riser. Often he would be up and out of the Mansion before any of the staff arrived. A typical Bellmon breakfast included a banana with several graham crackers, usually eaten on his way out the door.

Oklahoma's present governor, David Walters, is also an early riser. When he requests something special — more often than not — it is a fried egg sandwich on toast with mayonnaise and two strips of bacon.

Picture of Governor "Alfalfa Bill" Murray 1931-1935

This menu is perfect for an Easter brunch.

spring brunch

Passion Fruit Salad
Apple Sausage Loaf
Breakfast K Bobs
Hearty Ham Tarts
Salmon and Caviar Quiches

This letter from William H. Taft, 27th president of the United States, was written to Governor J.B.A. Robertson, who served Oklahoma from 1919 to 1923.

17

Passion Fruit Salad

½ cup sugar
1 cup water
2 tablespoons poppy seeds
2 limes, peeled and juiced
2 pounds strawberries, halved
12 kiwi fruit, peeled and sliced
12 passion fruit, halved, seeded, pulp removed and chopped
8 ounces seeded grapes, halved
Fresh mint, chopped

In a small saucepan, combine sugar, water, poppy seeds, and lime peel. Heat gently, stirring constantly, until sugar dissolves. Bring to boil for 2 to 3 minutes. Remove from heat and cool. In a medium-size bowl, mix fruits and sprinkle with chopped mint. Pour in syrup and lime juice and stir gently. 351 calories per serving. Serves 8.

Protein 3.9	Carbohydrate 87	Fat 2.42	Cholesterol 0

Apple Sausage Loaf

One of my favorite brunch foods!

½ package frozen puff pastry, 1 sheet
8 ounces lite pork sausage
1 egg, beaten
¾ cup chopped yellow onion
2 Granny Smith apples, very finely chopped
½ cup dried herb stuffing mix
1 egg, beaten for glaze
2 tablespoons water
3 tablespoons sesame seeds

Preheat oven to 400 degrees. Roll pastry to a 19 by 15 inch rectangle and cover with damp towel. In a large bowl, mix sausage, egg, onion, apples, and stuffing. Mix with hands to thoroughly combine.

Spoon sausage filling down center of pastry, leaving about 1¾ inches of pastry at top and bottom, and 4 inches on each side of filling. Brush edges of pastry with beaten egg mixed with water; fold top and bottom over filling. Make 3 inch cuts at 2 inch intervals down each side of the pastry. Fold 1 strip over filling from alternate sides until filling is completely enclosed. Fold top and bottom flaps over each other and pinch closed.

Brush with beaten egg and water mixture; sprinkle with sesame seeds. Place on baking sheet and bake 30 minutes, until golden. Serve hot or cold. 404 calories per serving. Serves 6.

Protein 11.8	Carbohydrates 40	Fat 23.3	Cholesterol 155

Breakfast K Bobs

24 slices bacon
4 ounces Swiss cheese
32 cherry tomatoes
32 button mushrooms
2 tablespoons olive oil
2 teaspoons tomato paste
1 teaspoon A1 Sauce
1 tablespoon Chinese hot mustard
1 teaspoon soy sauce
1 teaspoon Worcestershire sauce

Halve bacon slices; cut cheese into 48 cubes, and wrap cube with bacon. Place bacon rolls, mushrooms, and tomatoes on skewers, starting and ending with a bacon roll. In a bowl, mix together the remaining ingredients and brush over kabobs. Cover and marinate several hours, or overnight.

In a preheated broiler, place K Bobs on a cookie sheet and broil for 5 minutes, turning frequently, and brushing with remaining sauce. Serve immediately. 287 calories per serving. Serves 6 to 8.

Protein 14.8	Carbohydrate 7	Fat 22.7	Cholesterol 37

Hearty Ham Tarts

꩜

2 packages pie shell dough, 4 rounds
2 tablespoons dry mustard
Flour
8 ounces black forest ham or smoked, chopped
8 ounces big eye Swiss cheese, shredded
2 eggs, beaten
1⅓ cups half and half
Salt and pepper to taste
Grated nutmeg

Preheat oven to 400 degrees. Lay out pie dough rounds until room temperature. Sprinkle both sides with dry mustard and flour. Using a rolling pin, thin shells to half original thickness. Place individual tart pans on dough and cut dough approximately three-fourths inch larger than pans. Put dough inside shells and pat into place. Divide ham and cheese equally among shells.

In a medium size bowl, combine egg, half and half, salt, and pepper. Pour over ham and cheese and sprinkle with grated nutmeg. To protect oven from spillage, bake on a cookie sheet 25 minutes, or until golden and set. Serve warm. 523 calories per serving. Serves 8.

Protein 21.3   Carbohydrate 31   Fat 34.5   Cholesterol 127

Salmon and Caviar Quiches

꩜

½ package frozen puff pastry, thawed
6 eggs
1½ cups whipping cream
½ teaspoon salt
⅛ teaspoon nutmeg
¼ pound smoked salmon, chopped
4 ounces salmon caviar
Fresh dill sprigs

Preheat oven to 400 degrees. Grease twenty-four 2 inch tart pans or mini muffin tins. Unfold pastry sheets and place on a lightly floured board; roll out slightly, cut into 24 rounds, and place in the greased pans. In a bowl, beat eggs, cream, salt, and nutmeg until blended. Stir in half the chopped salmon. Spoon mixture into the pastry lined pans, distributing the salmon evenly. Sprinkle most of the remaining salmon in the filled cups, reserving some for garnish.

Bake 10 to 15 minutes or until filling is puffed and golden. Carefully remove from pans, and garnish with reserved salmon, caviar, and dill sprigs. Serve warm. If prepared ahead, remove quiches from pans, cool completely on racks, cover, and refrigerate. To reheat, arrange on baking sheets; bake in a 400 degree oven about 5 minutes until heated. 114 calories per serving. Makes 24 quiches.

Protein 4.2   Carbohydrate 3.06   Fat 9.6   Cholesterol 123

The U.S.S. Oklahoma Punchbowl, *displayed at the Mansion from 1975 to 1986,
is now permanently housed at the Oklahoma Historical Society.*

lunch

Donna Nigh, wife of former Governor George Nigh, served lunch to a most gracious guest.

Each year, George hosted a press luncheon for the working press which consisted of newspapers, radio, and TV. This particular day the luncheon was on a Wednesday, which was the day we had public open house at the Mansion. The luncheon was to be on the 3rd floor at 11:30 and open house began at 1 p.m. We all noticed a gentleman who was alone and no one seemed to know what station or paper he represented.

Upon completion of the luncheon, George stationed himself at the door to visit with everyone. The gentleman mentioned told George he sure enjoyed lunch, and was surprised to find out we served lunch every Wednesday for open house, and would sure tell his friends. Needless to say the guards were a little more careful the next time. They just assumed since the man arrived at 11:30 that he was part of the press corps and sent him upstairs.

The Governor and Mrs. George Nigh with children Mike and Georgeann.

Shawnee's Best Shortcakes and Chicken Pasta Salad.

by the pool

Chicken Pasta Salad
Cheddar Stuffed Loaf
Shawnee's Best Shortcakes

The Oklahoma-shaped pool has often been the center for casual entertainment at the Mansion.

At one party acknowledging the retirement of Attorney General Robert Henry, former Attorney General Mike Turpen used the edge of the diving board as the platform for his speech. While honoring Mr. Henry, Turpen lost his balance and fell into the pool, suit and all!

The Oklahoma-shaped pool was donated to the state by friends of Governor George and Donna Nigh, January 1979.

Cheddar Stuffed Loaf.

23

Chicken Pasta Salad

Serve with French bread or Cheddar Stuffed Loaf.

6   chicken breast halves, about 1½ pounds
1   onion, quartered
1   carrot, halved
1   celery stalk, halved
⅓   cup pine nuts
⅓   pound snow peas
1   teaspoon margarine
1   pound linguine
15   ounces garbanzo beans, cooked
½   pound fresh mushrooms, sliced
2   ounces stuffed green olives, drained
     and sliced
2   ounces pitted black olives, drained
     and sliced
1   red or green bell pepper,
     cut into strips
1   jar marinated artichoke hearts,
     drained

Boil chicken in water with onion, carrot, and celery until done. Cool. Remove chicken from stock, then skin, debone, and cut into bite size pieces. Sauté pine nuts in margarine until nuts begin to brown. Cool. Cook snow peas in boiling water for 1 minute. Cool in ice water and drain.

Cook linguine in stock until al dente. Drain linguine and rinse in cold water; discard stock. Mix chicken, pine nuts, peas, linguine, beans, mushrooms, olives, bell pepper, and artichoke hearts in large bowl and toss to blend thoroughly.

Dressing
1   cup olive oil
5   tablespoons red wine vinegar
½   cup minced parsley
4   teaspoons Dijon mustard
½   teaspoon curry powder
1½   teaspoons salt
1   teaspoon pepper
½   teaspoon garlic powder

To prepare dressing, mix all ingredients in a small bowl. Pour over salad and toss well. Refrigerate. Can be prepared a day ahead and refrigerated. 559 calories per serving. Serves 10 to 12.

| Protein 30 | Carbohydrate 33.6 | Fat 35 | Cholesterol 57 |

Cheddar Stuffed Loaf

This can be served with practically any luncheon salad — delicious, but not low cal.

1   large loaf French bread
¾   cup unsalted butter, softened
1   tablespoon thyme
1   teaspoon Tabasco®
½   cup freshly grated Parmesan cheese
½   cup thinly sliced Bermuda onions
2   cups grated sharp Cheddar cheese

Preheat oven to 400 degrees. Cut the bread lengthwise. Beat the butter with the thyme and Tabasco®, add Parmesan cheese. Spread mixture on each loaf. Place onions on the bottom slice and sprinkle evenly with Cheddar cheese. Cover with top slice and wrap securely in foil.

Bake for 25 minutes until crust is hard. Slice crosswise to serve. 507 calories per serving. Serves 8.

| Protein 22 | Carbohydrate 15.2 | Fat 42 | Cholesterol 119 |

Shawnee's Best Shortcakes

2   cups Shawnee Baking Mix; outside of Oklahoma, use Bisquick®
2   tablespoons shortening
2   tablespoons sugar
⅔   cup water
     Melted butter

Preheat oven to 450 degrees. Mix first four ingredients and roll out to ¾ inch thickness. Cut with biscuit cutter or in squares to preferred size. Brush tops with melted butter. Bake 10 to 12 minutes. 173 calories per serving. Serves 8.

Protein 3	Carbohydrate 25	Fat 6.6	Cholesterol 8.3

Former State Attorney General Robert Henry, while a Representative in the Oklahoma Legislature, took "floor privileges" to praise Oklahoma products. At the end of his extensive rambling, the chamber's entire presence was requested in the House Lounge.

Encouraged by Representative Henry, Shawnee Mills had baked shortcakes and provided huge, beautiful strawberries from Stilwell, Oklahoma. Strawberry Shortcakes were served to all! By a vote of unanimous consent Shawnee's Best Shortcakes became a part of the official daily House Journal record on May 15, 1985.

Shawnee's Best Shortcakes.

Casual Lunch served in sunroom.

casual lunch

Hearty Sausage Soup
Maggie Cake

Maggie Cake.

Hearty Sausage Soup

❧

Superb with pumpernickel bread and herb butter.

2 pounds Italian sausage links
2 cups dry white wine
2 cloves garlic, minced
1 large yellow onion, coarsely chopped
5 cups chopped cabbage
28 ounces stewed tomatoes and juice
1 cup water
4 ounces green chili peppers, rinsed, seeded and chopped

With fork tines, prick sausage casing several times. Cut into 1 inch pieces, place in a large bowl, and add wine and garlic. Marinate for 1 hour. Drain sausage pieces, reserving the marinade.

In a Dutch oven or kettle with a lid, cook the sausage and onion until the meat is brown and the onion is tender; drain off fat. Add reserved marinade. Bring to boil; reduce heat and simmer, covered, 20 minutes. Stir in cabbage, tomatoes and juice, water, and peppers. Simmer covered for 20 more minutes, stirring occasionally.

As good as this soup is when first made, it is even better refrigerated and reheated the next day. 733 calories per serving. Serves 8.

Protein 42   Carbohydrate 12.6   Fat 52   Cholesterol 156

Maggie Cake

❧

Senator David L. Boren, former governor of Oklahoma, and his wife, Molly Shi Boren, served this cake often while Mansion residents. Named for a lifelong friend of Mrs. Boren's parents, Maggie Prather of Stratford, Oklahoma, this recipe has been a family favorite for many, many years.

1 cup butter
2½ cups sugar
5 egg yolks, beaten
1 cup buttermilk
5 teaspoons coffee instant granules
3 cups flour
1 teaspoon baking powder
1 teaspoon soda
4 teaspoons cocoa
1 teaspoon salt
2 teaspoons vanilla
5 egg whites, stiffly beaten

Icing
3 teaspoons coffee
1 egg
½ cup butter
2 teaspoons cocoa
1 teaspoon vanilla
  Dash of salt
1 pound powdered sugar
  Heavy whipping cream as needed
4 ounces Oklahoma pecans

Preheat oven to 350 degrees. Mix all ingredients adding the egg whites last. Bake for 15 to 20 minutes in two 9 inch cake pans. For the icing, combine first six ingredients in a mixing bowl. While mixing, gradually add sugar and cream, as needed, to make the right consistency for spreading. Decorate with pecans. 447 calories per serving. Serves 20.

Protein 4.9   Carbohydrate 58   Fat 22.6   Cholesterol 131

Hearty Sausage Soup.

Swordfish Steak and vegetables on grill.

business lunch

Spinach Salad with Feta Vinaigrette
Swordfish Steaks with Pineapple Salsa
Pecan Rice Pilaf
Carrot Cake

Spinach Salad with Feta Vinaigrette.

Spinach Salad with Feta Vinaigrette

1   pound fresh spinach, washed, picked, and dried
6   fresh mushrooms, sliced
1   Bermuda onion, sliced paper thin
1   cup seasoned croutons
½   cup crumbled feta cheese

Dressing
⅓   cup canola oil
⅓   cup red wine vinegar
1   tablespoon vinegar
2   teaspoons fresh thyme
1   teaspoon chopped fresh oregano
1   teaspoon chopped fresh garlic
1   tablespoon coarsely ground pepper
2   tablespoons freshly squeezed lemon juice
1   tablespoon finely chopped shallots
1   teaspoon coarsely ground prepared mustard
¼   cup crumbled feta cheese

Place spinach in a large bowl and toss in mushrooms and onions. Mix all dressing ingredients and add enough to lightly coat salad. Divide among 6 chilled salad plates. Sprinkle with feta cheese and croutons. Serve immediately. 250 calories per serving. Serves 6.

Protein 7.9	Carbohydrate 13	Fat 19	Cholesterol 25

Swordfish Steaks with Pineapple Salsa

Great for a light luncheon menu served with Pecan Rice Pilaf.

4   stalks celery
5   carrots
4   baking potatoes, unpeeled
3   medium size zucchini
1   large leek, halved lengthwise
2   large onions, unpeeled
1   whole head garlic, crushed
1   pound mushrooms
2   teaspoons coarse ground pepper
1   tablespoon dried thyme
½   cup parsley, stems included
4   bay leaves
2   cups dry white table wine

Cut up celery, carrots, potatoes, zucchini, leek, and onions. In a large stockpot, combine vegetables and remaining ingredients, add water to cover. Bring to a boil, reduce heat, cover, and simmer 1 hour. Remove cover, simmer 45 minutes. Pour vegetable mixture through strainer, pressing vegetables to remove excess stock. Discard vegetables. Makes about 8 cups. Freezes well.

8   swordfish steaks, about 1 inch thick
     Salt and white pepper
2   bunches cilantro, washed, reserve 8 sprigs for garnish
½   cup fresh lemon juice
1   tablespoon crushed red pepper
½   cup grated gingerroot
3   tablespoons garlic paste

Salt and pepper both sides of swordfish and place in shallow dish. Mix the remaining ingredients with the vegetable stock and pour over fish. Cover and marinate at least 2 hours at room temperature, or overnight in the refrigerator, turning several times. Prepare salsa.

Pineapple Salsa

2   small pineapples
1   jalapeño pepper, seeded and minced
8   sprigs cilantro, reserved from stock recipe

Approximately 2 hours before serving, peel and finely chop pineapple. In a serving bowl, combine pineapple, jalapeño pepper, and reserved chopped cilantro. Prepare outdoor grill. Place fish on grill and cook 7 to 9 minutes on each side until fish is lightly browned and flakes with a fork. Garnish each steak with cilantro and serve with salsa. 536 calories per serving. Serves 8.

Protein 49	Carbohydrate 55	Fat 10.1	Cholesterol 86

Pecan Rice Pilaf

1   cup pecans
1   tablespoon margarine
3   cups hot cooked rice
    Salt and pepper to taste

Preheat oven to 250 degrees. Place pecan halves in a single layer on baking sheet and toast 15 minutes or until golden. Chop pecans coarsely and set aside. Melt margarine in skillet and add pecans, stirring to coat. Add rice, salt, and pepper; toss with pecans. 254 calories per serving. Serves 6.

Protein 4.2	Carbohydrate 27.5	Fat 15	Cholesterol 0

Carrot Cake

2   cups sifted cake flour
2   cups sugar
2   teaspoons baking soda
2   teaspoons cinnamon
1   teaspoon salt
½   cup oil
3   eggs
1   cup applesauce
3   cups grated carrots
1   teaspoon vanilla

Icing

1   stick butter
8   ounces cream cheese, softened
1   box powdered sugar
1   cup chopped pecans
1   teaspoon vanilla

Preheat oven to 350 degrees. In a mixing bowl, blend flour, sugar, soda, cinnamon, salt, and oil. Add eggs, one at a time, then applesauce, carrots, and vanilla. Divide batter between two 9 inch greased cake pans and bake for 30 minutes. For the icing, combine butter and cream cheese; add sugar, pecans, vanilla. Mix until smooth, and ice cake. 485 calories per serving. Serves 15.

Protein 4.5	Carbohydrate 69	Fat 22.3	Cholesterol 88

The glass hat sculpture belonged to Governor George Nigh, who served from 1979 to 1987.
The glass elephant was a favorite of Governor Henry Bellmon, Oklahoma's first Republican Governor.

summertime menu

Chilled Asparagus Soup with Coriander Salsa
Marinated Broccoli Salad
Tropical K Bobs
Cold Grapefruit Soufflé

The ticket admits one to a lecture by David L. Payne, leader of the Boomer Movement, which opened the Unassigned Lands to settlement on April 22, 1889.

Tropical K Bobs and Marinated Broccoli Salad.

35

Chilled Asparagus Soup with Coriander Salsa

If fat content is not an issue, two avocados substituted for the asparagus make a truly wonderful dish.

2   cans asparagus spears, drained
4   teaspoons fresh lemon juice
4   teaspoons fresh lime juice
1⅓ cups light cream
2   cups chicken stock
     Salt and pepper

Whir the asparagus in a food processor. Add lemon and lime juices, and whir again. Transfer mixture to a strainer lined with gauze and drain all juice. Return to food processor and puree until smooth. Add cream and enough chicken stock for a creamy consistency. Transfer to a bowl, cover, and chill at least 4 hours.

Coriander Salsa
2   small tomatoes, peeled, seeded, and chopped
1   2-inch piece cucumber, peeled, seeded, and chopped
½   red bell pepper, seeded and chopped
1   jalapeño or to taste, seeded and minced
2   scallions, minced
1   small clove garlic, minced
1   tablespoon minced fresh coriander
2   slices bacon, fried and crumbled

Excluding the bacon, combine all ingredients in food processor till blended. Let stand at least 15 minutes at room temperature. Recipe can be made a few hours ahead.

Ladle soup into four chilled bowls, and serve with a spoonful of salsa in the center of each bowl, topped with a healthy sprinkle of chopped bacon. 333 calories per serving. Serves 4.

Protein 10.3   Carbohydrate 14.4   Fat 28   Cholesterol 92

Marinated Broccoli Salad

3   bunches broccoli
1   tablespoon chicken bullion, granulated
1   cup baby carrots, peeled
1   cup cider vinegar
1   tablespoon sugar
1   tablespoon dill weed
1   teaspoon salt
1   teaspoon pepper
1   teaspoon garlic salt
1½ cups vegetable oil

Cut broccoli into florets and place in a microwave safe bowl with ¼ cup hot water and bullion. Cover with plastic wrap and cook on high for about 5 minutes, until crisp-tender. Remove broccoli and cool. In the same bowl, add the carrots and microwave, covered, for approximately 5 minutes until crisp-tender. Remove and cool. Mix all remaining ingredients in a large bowl. Add broccoli and carrots and marinate at least 24 hours.

Serve on a lettuce lined plate. 519 calories per serving. Serves 6 to 8.

Protein 1.84   Carbohydrate 9   Fat 55   Cholesterol 167

Tropical K Bobs

½   cup lite soy sauce
½   cup unsweetened pineapple juice
¼   cup canola oil
2   tablespoons brown sugar
1   tablespoon garlic, minced
2   teaspoons fresh ginger, grated
1   teaspoon dry mustard
¼   teaspoon ground pepper
1½ pounds chicken breasts, boneless, skinned, and cut in 1 inch cubes
18   cherry tomatoes
1   large red bell pepper, cut into 1 inch cubes

12	medium mushrooms
15	ounces pineapple chunks, unsweetened and drained
3	cups cooked rice, hot

In a saucepan, combine first 8 ingredients; bring to a boil, reduce heat, and simmer 5 minutes. Let cool. Pour mixture into shallow dish and add chicken, tossing to coat. Cover and marinate in refrigerator at least 1 hour. Remove chicken from marinade, reserving liquid. Alternate chicken, tomatoes, peppers, mushrooms, and pineapple chunks on skewers. Grill over hot coals for 20 minutes or until done, turning and basting frequently with marinade. Serve over hot rice. 489 calories per serving. Serves 6.

| Protein 41 | Carbohydrate 49 | Fat 1 | Cholesterol 94 |

Cold Grapefruit Soufflé

༚

*Don't let the name fool you –
has a very light refreshing taste.*

4	large grapefruits
2	packages gelatin
½	cup Triple Sec Liqueur
6	eggs, separated
1¼	cups granulated sugar
1⅓	cups half and half
1⅓	cups heavy cream
	Pinch of salt
	Pinch of cream of tartar
1	cup heavy cream
	Mint leaves

Working over a bowl to catch juice, peel and section the grapefruits. Press pulp through a strainer to yield 2 cups of grapefruit juice. Discard the membranes. In a heat proof bowl, sprinkle gelatin over the Triple Sec and let sit until spongy. Place the bowl in a pan of simmering water until the gelatin is completely dissolved. In a large bowl, lightly whisk the egg yolks with 1 cup of the sugar.

In a heavy saucepan, heat the light cream with two-thirds cup grapefruit juice. Gradually whisk the hot cream into the yolk mixture. Return it to the pan and cook over medium heat, stirring with a wooden spoon, until the mixture thickens sufficiently to coat the back of a spoon, about 3 minutes. Do not boil or it will curdle.

Strain this mixture; whisk in the dissolved gelatin and remaining grapefruit juice. Set the bowl over a pan of ice and stir occasionally with a rubber spatula while the mixture chills.

Beat the egg whites and, after 20 seconds, add the salt and cream of tartar. Sprinkle in 3 tablespoons sugar as the whites thicken and continue beating until stiff peaks form. Beat the heavy cream to stiff peaks. When the grapefruit mixture is nearly set, fold in most of the whipped cream, reserving ⅔ cup for decoration. Fold in beaten egg whites. Spoon mixture into bowls and refrigerate.

Just before serving, decorate each soufflé with a rosette of whipped cream and top with mint leaves. 637 calories per serving. Serves 6 to 8.

| Protein 9 | Carbohydrate 65 | Fat 35 | Cholesterol 319 |

Picture of Governor and Mrs. Walters with their children at Inaugural Ball, 1991.

ladies' luncheon

Cool Carrot and Curry Soup
Oyster Caesar Salad
Coconut Custard

Cool Carrot and Curry Soup served in state china soup tureen.

39

Cool Carrot and Curry Soup

❦

2   onions, sliced thinly
6   carrots, about 3 cups, sliced thinly
1½ tablespoons canola oil
2   teaspoons curry powder
2   cups chicken broth
4   cups water
     Sour cream
     Fresh chives, chopped

In a large heavy saucepan, cook the onions and carrots in the oil, covered, over moderately low heat. Stir occasionally. When the onions are softened, add the curry powder and cook 1 minute. Add the broth and water, bring to a boil and simmer for 15 to 20 minutes, or until the carrots are very tender. Puree in food processor in batches. Chill covered until cool. Can be made a day in advance. Divide the soup among 6 bowls, and garnish with a dollop of sour cream and chopped chives. 92 calories per serving. Serves 6.

Protein 3	Carbohydrate 6	Fat 6.6	Cholesterol 5.3

Oyster Caesar Salad

❦

A favorite of mine after Mansion Administrator Steven Bunch brought the recipe back from New Orleans.

3   dozen oysters, shucked
1   cup flour
     Salt and coarse black pepper
3   cloves garlic
3   eggs
½   cup skim milk
2   cups Italian seasoned bread crumbs
¼   cup grated Parmesan cheese
3   heads romaine lettuce

Drain oysters. Mix the flour, 1½ teaspoons salt and ½ teaspoon pepper. Mash the garlic with a pinch of salt. In a large bowl, whisk the garlic paste with the eggs, milk, ½ teaspoon salt and ½ teaspoon pepper. In a medium sized bowl, mix bread crumbs and Parmesan cheese. Dredge the oysters in flour, dip in the egg mixture, and then coat with bread crumbs. Place oysters on a baking sheet in a single layer. Refrigerate until ready to fry. Wash and dry the lettuce and tear into bite-size pieces.

Dressing

2   cloves garlic, mashed
2   anchovy fillets or ½ teaspoon anchovy paste
1   cup grated Parmesan cheese
2   lemons, juiced
½   teaspoon white wine vinegar
1   tablespoon no fat mayonnaise
½   cup olive oil
2   tablespoons coarse mustard
2   tablespoons Worcestershire sauce
     Salt and pepper to taste

Mash the garlic, anchovy fillets, and a pinch of salt into a fine paste. Add ⅔ cup cheese, ½ cup lemon juice, vinegar, and mayonnaise. Whisk in the olive oil, mustard, and Worcestershire sauce. Season with salt and pepper.

Heat oil to 350 degrees for frying. Toss lettuce with dressing. Divide salad among 6 plates. Fry breaded oysters in batches until golden and crisp, about 10 seconds per side. Drain oysters, sprinkle with salt, and place them on the dressed lettuce. Sprinkle with the remaining ⅓ cup cheese. Serve at once. 800 calories per serving. Serves 6.

Protein 50	Carbohydrate 62	Fat 38	Cholesterol 332

Coconut Custard

⤜⧽⧼⤛

⅓ cup sugar
3 large egg yolks
⅔ cup grated or flaked coconut
2 cups milk, warmed
   Pinch of salt
1 teaspoon vanilla
6 tablespoons apricot preserves, warmed

Preheat oven to 350 degrees. Beat sugar and egg yolks in a mixing bowl with a mixer. Add coconut, milk, salt, and vanilla; blend well. Pour mixture into custard cups; place in baking pan. Add warm water to cover sides of cups. Place on lower shelf of oven and bake until knife set in the custard comes out almost clean, 30 to 35 minutes. After the custard has cooled slightly, spread with preserves. 244 calories per serving. Serves 6.

Protein 4.9   Carbohydrate 30   Fat 12.5   Cholesterol 148

Oyster Caesar Salad.

41

The gavel was a gift to Governor William J. Holloway, who served from 1929-1931, from George Shirk, mayor of Oklahoma City at the time.

working lunch

Italian Herbed Tuna Sandwiches
Chocolate Pudding Cake

Governor Walters often works through lunch.
This book, *Building a Better Oklahoma, a*
Comprehensive Transportation Plan for Oklahoma,
was a product of one of those lunches.

Chocolate Pudding Cake.

Italian Herbed Tuna Sandwiches

This unusual tuna sandwich was served to unsuspecting guests working through lunch at the Mansion — their reviews were quite favorable!

½	cup balsamic vinegar
1	tablespoon anchovy paste or equal amount of fillets, patted dry and minced
1	tablespoon mashed garlic
	Salt and pepper to taste
1	cup extra virgin olive oil
2	8 inch round loaves of crusty bread
2	cups thinly sliced radishes
2	cups loosely packed fresh basil
1	cup minced onion, soaked in water for 10 minutes and drained well
13	ounces tuna in oil, drained, and flaked
4	tomatoes, thinly sliced

In a bowl, whisk together the vinegar, anchovies, garlic, salt, and pepper. Add the oil in a stream, and whisk dressing until emulsified. Halve the bread horizontally and hollow out, leaving one-half inch thick shells. Spoon and spread one-fourth of the dressing into each half.

Working with one loaf at a time, arrange half the radishes in the bottom shell, top it with ½ cup of the basil, and sprinkle with half the onion. Arrange half the tuna on the onion, then another layer of ½ cup of the basil, and top with tomatoes. Fit the top shell over the tomatoes. Assemble another sandwich with the remaining bread, radishes, basil, onions, tuna, and tomatoes in the same manner. Wrap the sandwiches in plastic wrap and put in a jelly-roll pan or cookie sheet. Top the sandwiches with a baking sheet and a large bowl filled with several 2 pound weights. Chill for at least one hour, no more than four. Cut into fourths and serve 4 hungry people. 884 calories per serving.

Protein 34	Carbohydrate 41	Fat 67	Cholesterol 60

Chocolate Pudding Cake

1	cup all purpose flour
¾	cup sugar
2	tablespoons cocoa powder
2	teaspoons baking powder
½	teaspoon salt
½	cup skim milk
2	tablespoons oil
1	teaspoon vanilla
¾	cup brown sugar
¼	cup cocoa powder
1¾	cups hot water

Preheat oven to 350 degrees. Sift flour, sugar, cocoa powder, baking powder, and salt in a mixing bowl. Stir in milk, oil, and vanilla; blend well. Spray an 8 inch square baking pan with nonstick spray and add batter. Combine last three ingredients and pour over batter. Bake for 45 minutes. 249 calories per serving. Serves 8.

Protein 2.7	Carbohydrate 51	Fat 4.4	Cholesterol .25

The Mansion's second floor deck off the family room overlooks the South Lawn.

Formal Living Room, 1991.

afternoon tea

Indian Tea
Cucumber Tea Sandwiches
Maraschino Delights
Lemon Honey Pecan Muffins
Peach Almond Butter
Poppy Seed Bread
Cinnamon Tea Muffins

*This tea set was a gift from Governor Walters to his wife
following a diplomatic trip to Russia in 1991.*

Indian Tea

4	lemons, juiced with rinds
2	cups water
2½	cups sugar
1	cup strong tea
¼	teaspoon ground cloves
4	tablespoons lemon juice
2	tablespoons lime juice
1	teaspoon almond extract
1	quart ginger ale or Sprite®

Heat lemon rinds with 2 cups water. Dissolve sugar in water, remove the rinds, and add tea, cloves, lemon and lime juices. Cool. Immediately before serving, add almond extract and ginger ale. Serve over crushed ice. Serves 16.

Cucumber Tea Sandwiches

8	slices of bread, any type or mixed Boursin Cheese with herbs
1	cucumber, thinly sliced

Spread cheese on bread and top with cucumber slices. Remove crusts and cut each sandwich into triangles. 166 calories per serving. Serves 8.

Protein 4.15   Carbohydrate 13   Fat 11   Cholesterol 30

Other Ideas for tea sandwiches —
•Diced chutney and almonds, and cream cheese;
•½ cup of chopped raisins and chopped walnuts blended with 1 cup cream cheese and a little heavy cream;
•¾ cup of chopped stuffed olives and walnuts;
•About 1½ cups chopped stuffed green olives blended with ½ cup cream cheese. Garnish with sprig of fresh parsley;
•½ cup of each, chopped preserved ginger and walnuts, spread on nut bread and topped with sliced bananas.

Maraschino Delights

¾	cup shortening
1	teaspoon vanilla
1	cup brown sugar
1	egg
¼	cup chopped maraschino cherries
½	cup chopped nuts
2	cups flour
½	teaspoon soda
½	teaspoon salt
½	teaspoon cream of tartar

In a mixing bowl, blend shortening, vanilla, sugar, and egg. Add cherries and nuts, and mix in flour, baking soda, salt, and cream of tartar. Roll dough into two rolls, wrap in wax paper, and chill in icebox. Preheat oven to 400 degrees. When chilled, slice and bake for 10 to 12 minutes. 99 calories per serving. Yields 3 dozen cookies.

Protein .98   Carbohydrate 11.4   Fat 5.7   Cholesterol 7.6

Lemon Honey Pecan Muffins

Best served with Peach Almond Butter.

2	teaspoons baking soda
1½	cups buttermilk
1	cup or 2 sticks butter, softened
1½	cups honey
4	eggs
4	cups all purpose flour
2	tablespoons grated lemon rind
½	cup chopped pecans
	Sugar and cinnamon

Preheat oven to 375 degrees. Combine baking soda and buttermilk in small non-metallic bowl. In a large bowl, beat butter and honey together, then beat in eggs, one at a time. Gradually fold in the flour, followed by the buttermilk mixture, the lemon rind, and nuts. Do not overmix. Spoon mixture into greased miniature muffin tins and sprinkle surface with sugar and cinnamon mixture. Bake for 12 to 15 minutes. 124 calories per serving. Yields 4 dozen miniature muffins.

Protein 1.96   Carbohydrate 17.3   Fat 5.6   Cholesterol 34

Peach Almond Butter

1	cup or 2 sticks butter, softened
1	tablespoon powdered sugar
2	large peaches, very ripe, peeled, and finely chopped
¼	teaspoon ground cinnamon
⅛	teaspoon nutmeg
¼	cup toasted almonds

Combine all the ingredients, except the almonds, in a mixing bowl. Mound the butter into a fancy dish and garnish with nuts; cover and refrigerate. Serve at room temperature. 42 calories per serving. Serves 48 miniature muffins.

Protein .17   Carbohydrate .65   Fat 4.4   Cholesterol 11

Poppy Seed Bread

3	cups flour
1½	cups milk
½	teaspoon salt
1⅛	cups oil
1½	teaspoons baking powder
3	eggs
1½	teaspoons poppy seed
1½	teaspoons almond extract
1½	teaspoons vanilla
2¼	cups sugar
1	teaspoon butter flavoring

Preheat oven to 350 degrees. Mix ingredients thoroughly, and pour into greased and floured loaf pans. Bake for 1 hour.

Glaze

¼	cup orange juice
¾	cup sugar
¾	teaspoon almond extract
¾	teaspoon butter flavoring
¾	teaspoon vanilla extract

Mix ingredients with a fork and pour over cake. Better the second day than the first, this bread freezes well for months. 508 calories per serving. Yields 2 loaves.

Protein 5.6   Carbohydrate 68   Fat 23.4   Cholesterol 71

Cinnamon Tea Muffins

1½	cups plus 2 tablespoons flour
¾	cup sugar
2	teaspoons baking powder
¼	teaspoon salt
¼	teaspoon nutmeg
⅓	cup butter, melted
½	cup milk
1	egg, beaten
⅓	cup butter, melted
1	teaspoon cinnamon
½	cup sugar

Preheat oven to 400 degrees. Combine first five ingredients. Add ⅓ cup melted butter, milk, and egg; mix thoroughly. Grease and flour small muffin tins and fill each cup half full. Bake for 20 minutes, or until lightly browned. Remove from pans immediately; dip in remaining ⅓ cup melted butter and roll in mixture of sugar and cinnamon. Serve warm. 353 calories per serving. Serves 8.

Protein 3.8   Carbohydrate 45   Fat 17.6   Cholesterol 79

Faux pastries from the Tulsa Flea Market always tempt visitors in the Mansion kitchen.

dinner

So many of the memorable occasions Donna Nigh, wife of former Governor George Nigh, remembers from her eight years of living in the mansion revolve around food functions.

Feeding large groups of people can be very trying and at the same time provide lots of laughs. Most of the time is spent organizing social events. You sometimes feel like a caterer and inn-keeper. It's fun to reflect on events that may not have been too humorous at the time but now they are.

We were entertaining Speaker and Mrs. Carl Albert at a dinner party. Everything went fine until the caterer put a chocolate soufflé into the oven and did not realize the oven door lock was for automatic cleaning and did not open until the cycle was over. The mansion filled with smoke and our soufflé was charred. Fortunately, I had baked a birthday cake for our nephew that day so we did have dessert with all the smoke alarms going off.

Only the hors d'eouvres are edible.

51

Statue of Will Rogers is an exact replica of the one that stands in the nation's capitol.

buffet dinner

Sicilian Salad
Wine Basted Tenderloin
Wild Rice with Currants and Scallions
Braised Celery
Pear Mincemeat Tart

Oklahoma's last Territorial Governor, Frank Frantz, 1906-1907, photographed with Osage Indians. The Silver Star Medal was from the Spanish American War's Battle of San Juan Hill.

David L. Payne wrote this card while leader of the Oklahoma Boomer Movement. The spoon belonged to Oklahoma Territory's Governor William C. Renfrow, who served from 1893 to 1897.

53

Sicilian Salad

❧

2	heads romaine lettuce
2	oranges, peeled, membrane removed
2¼	cups sliced black olives
¼	cup orange juice
2	teaspoons red wine vinegar
½	teaspoon salt
2	tablespoons paprika
¼	cup olive oil
¼	cup finely chopped walnuts

Wash, de-rib, and tear salad into bite size pieces. Drain well and place in large bowl. Thinly slice oranges crosswise and lay over salad; sprinkle sliced olives on top. In a jar with a lid, combine the remaining ingredients and shake well. Spoon over salad. 204 calories per serving. Serves 6.

Protein 4.4   Carbohydrate 10.8   Fat 16.5   Cholesterol 0

Wine Basted Tenderloin

❧

3-4	pound tenderloin, trimmed
	Coarse ground pepper
8	tablespoons butter
½	cup chopped green onions
1	cup sliced fresh mushrooms
1½	cups dry sherry
2	tablespoons soy sauce
1	tablespoon Dijon mustard

Preheat oven to 400 degrees. Generously pepper the tenderloin, place in an oven proof pan, and dab 4 tablespoons of butter on top. Bake for 20 minutes. Over medium heat, sauté the green onions in remaining butter for several minutes. Add mushrooms and sauté until softened. Add the sherry, soy sauce, and pepper, and bring to boil. Remove from heat.

Carefully, to avoid smoke and splatters, pour sauce over tenderloin. Reduce oven temperature to 300 degrees and cook 20 to 30 minutes to desired doneness. Remove from oven and let stand 5 minutes before slicing. Serve with sauce from pan. 1065 calories per serving. Serves 6.

Protein 90   Carbohydrate 51   Fat 37   Cholesterol 292

Wild Rice with Currants and Scallions

❧

1	large onion, chopped
2	tablespoons olive oil
2	cups wild rice, rinsed and drained
5	cups chicken broth
½	cup currants
	Salt to taste
1	bunch scallions, sliced diagonally

In a sauce pan, cook the onion in the oil over low heat, stirring until softened. Add rice and coat with oil. Add chicken broth and bring to a boil. Stir in the currants and salt; simmer covered for 20 minutes until rice is tender. Drain rice mixture and transfer to a bowl. Add the scallions. Pack rice mixture into a 7 cup ring mold and invert onto a platter. 114 calories per serving. Serves 6 to 10.

Protein 2.55   Carbohydrate 18.7   Fat 3.7   Cholesterol 0

Braised Celery

❧

1½	bunches of celery with leaves
2	tablespoons vegetable oil
1	tablespoon butter
	Salt to taste
1	teaspoon sugar
1	teaspoon celery seeds
⅓	cup chicken broth

Reserve the celery leaves and cut the stalks diagonally into slices one-eighth inch thick. In a heavy skillet, heat the oil and butter over moderately high heat until the oil is hot but not smoking. Sauté the celery, salt, sugar, and celery seeds, stirring constantly for 1 minute. Add the broth and celery leaves, bring to a boil, and simmer, covered, for 3 to 5 minutes or until the celery is crisp-tender. 59 calories per serving. Serves 8.

Protein .82   Carbohydrate 3.5   Fat 5.2   Cholesterol 4.2

Pear Mincemeat Tart

2	pears, firm, peeled and cored
¼	cup raisins
⅓	cup brown sugar
½	cup dry white wine
¼	teaspoon cinnamon
⅛	teaspoon ground cloves
¼	teaspoon nutmeg
¼	teaspoon ground ginger
2	tablespoons butter
1	tablespoon brandy

For the pear mincemeat, combine in a saucepan pears, raisins, sugar, and wine. Bring to a boil and simmer, partially covered, until pears are tender and liquid is reduced by half, about 40 minutes. Add cinnamon, cloves, nutmeg, ginger, butter, and brandy. Cook 5 more minutes. Mincemeat can be made ahead of time and stored in the refrigerator up to 5 days.

Glaze
¼	cup ginger preserves
5	pears, firm, peeled and cored
1	teaspoon water
½	lemon, juiced
2	tablespoons sugar
1	teaspoon brandy
1	cup heavy cream

For crust, make the glaze first. Heat ginger preserves with water over low heat until dissolved. Cut pears lengthwise into ¼ inch slices. Cover with juice and toss.

Sweet Pastry Crust
1¼	cups all purpose flour
¼	cup cake flour
¼	cup sugar
¼	teaspoon salt
¼	pound butter, chilled
2	egg yolks
3	tablespoons water

Mix the flours, sugar, and salt in a bowl. Using table knives, cut butter into mixture until it resembles coarse meal. Add egg yolks, and water, if necessary, to hold dough together. Press the dough into a ball, cover with plastic wrap, and chill at least 20 minutes before rolling out. Dough can be refrigerated for a few days but should be room temperature before rolling.

On a floured work surface, roll out pastry slightly larger than a 9 inch tart pan. Gently press dough into pan. Press the dough down around the sides until a fraction of an inch overlaps the edge. To trim crust, roll over top of pan with a rolling pin. Prick bottom of the shell. Chill 15 minutes.

Preheat oven to 375 degrees. Spread mincemeat on bottom of crust. Arrange pear slices in concentric circles, starting from outside edge and overlapping slightly to form 2 or 3 rings of pear slices, using smaller slices toward the center of tart. Sprinkle with 1½ tablespoons sugar. Bake until crust is golden brown and pears are tender, about 1 hour. Cool.

Brush glaze over cooled tart. Whip the cream with the remaining sugar and brandy. Serve with a dollop of whipped cream on the side. Sprinkle with grated nutmeg, if desired. 311 calories per serving. Serves 8.

Protein 1.4   Carbohydrate 44   Fat 14.8   Cholesterol 50

Casual dinner on the South Veranda.

kristen's favorite menu

Spinach Salad with Mandarin Oranges
Marinated Chicken Breasts with Rice Pilaf
Sherried Green Beans
Banana Pudding

*When our middle daughter is asked what she would like for
dinner, she always requests this menu.*

*Pocket watch, chain, and pen knife, worn by George Washington
Steele, 1st Territorial Governor appointed by President Harrison,
term 1890-1891.*

Spinach Salad with Mandarin Oranges

꧁꧂

This is one of the children's favorite recipes — great served with popovers to round out a meal.

2   pounds fresh spinach
2   cans mandarin oranges, drained
1   package almonds, shaved
½   Bermuda onion, sliced into thin rings

Wash, pick, and trim spinach; spin or pat dry. In a large salad bowl, layer spinach, oranges, onions, and dressing, using all ingredients.

Orange Poppy Seed Dressing
½   teaspoon finely grated orange zest
¼   teaspoon finely grated lemon zest
½   cup orange juice
1   tablespoon plus 1 teaspoon powdered fruit pectin
2   tablespoons honey
½   teaspoon poppy seeds

In a small mixing bowl, combine orange and lemon zest, orange juice, pectin, honey, and poppy seeds. Cover and refrigerate for several hours or overnight before using. Keeps in the refrigerator up to 3 days. 176 calories per serving. Serves 6.

Protein 5.4   Carbohydrate 20.3   Fat 10   Cholesterol 0

Marinated Chicken Breasts with Seasoned Rice Pilaf

꧁꧂

3   cups pineapple juice
⅔   cup sugar
¾   cup soy sauce
1½   teaspoons garlic powder
1   cup dry sherry
1½   teaspoons powdered ginger
½   cup red wine vinegar
2   boxes of seasoned rice mix
12   chicken breasts, boned

Mix all ingredients and pour just enough over chicken breasts to cover. Marinate at least 12 hours or overnight, and cook over charcoal grill. For the rice pilaf, add enough water to the remaining marinade to make 4 cups. Prepare the rice according to directions, using only one package of seasoning. 930 calories per serving. Serves 6 to 8.

Protein 61   Carbohydrate 117   Fat 8.4   Cholesterol 150

Sherried Green Beans

2 pounds frozen green beans
4 tablespoons butter
¼ cup lite soy sauce
⅔ cup dry sherry, not cooking sherry

Squeeze excess water from green beans and set aside. In a large skillet with lid, melt butter over medium heat. Add the remaining ingredients and stir. Cook covered over a medium to low flame approximately 20 to 30 minutes, stirring until beans are very tender. Add small amounts of water if necessary. Transfer to a warm bowl and serve immediately. 107 calories per serving. Serves 6.

Protein 2.3   Carbohydrate 9.6   Fat 4.1   Cholesterol 0

Banana Pudding

2 cups skim milk
2 egg yolks, beaten
⅔ cup sugar
5-6 tablespoons flour
⅛ teaspoon salt
1 tablespoon margarine
1 tablespoon vanilla
24-30 vanilla wafers
2-3 bananas, sliced

Combine milk and egg yolks in a saucepan, and heat over medium heat. Combine remaining sugar, flour, and salt; gradually add to milk mixture. Stir constantly until thickened. Remove from heat; add margarine and vanilla. Line an 8 inch square dish with vanilla wafers and bananas. Pour half of the pudding on top, repeat with a layer of vanilla wafers and bananas and top with remaining pudding. Crush 3 or 4 vanilla wafers across top of pudding. Serve warm or chilled. 314 calories per serving. Serves 6.

Protein 6   Carbohydrate 57   Fat 7.7   Cholesterol 107

Picture of Governor and Mrs. Walters, displayed in study at Mansion, was taken by the Walters' oldest daughter, Tanna, on a family vacation at Grand Lake.

Governor Johnston Murray wore these boots while in office from 1951 to 1955.

south lawn dinner with friends

Do's Skillet Fried Corn
Grilled Okra and Onions
Southern Oven Brisket
Summer Lime Pie

Do's Skillet Fried Corn, Grilled Okra and Onions,
and Southern Oven Brisket.

Do's Skillet Fried Corn

꧁꧂

2 tablespoons butter
¼ green bell pepper, finely chopped
¼ red bell pepper, finely chopped
 Corn from 12 cobs
½ cup half and half
1 tablespoon sugar
 Salt and pepper to taste

Melt the butter in a large skillet. When it begins to bubble, add the bell peppers and sauté approximately 3 to 5 minutes, until slightly softened. Mix in corn and sauté over medium heat for 6 minutes to heat thoroughly and cook corn. Add the half and half until corn is lightly coated, but not too saucy. Add sugar, salt, and pepper. 226 calories per serving. Serves 6 to 8.

Protein 6.4   Carbohydrate 37   Fat 8.6   Cholesterol 19

Grilled Okra and Onions

꧁꧂

2 pounds tender small okra pods, washed
1 pound yellow onions, peeled, quartered, sliced ½ inch thick
3 tablespoons minced fresh garlic
3 lemons, juiced
 Salt and pepper to taste
¼ cup extra virgin olive oil

Preheat the grill. With a paring knife, remove the okra stem parts of the pods and any discolored tips. Be very careful not to cut into the pod cavity. Place okra and onions in a shallow baking dish. In a small bowl, combine the garlic, lemon juice, salt, pepper, and olive oil. Stir to emulsify. Toss with okra and onions to coat. Marinate at least 2 hours, stirring occasionally.

Cover the rack of the grill with aluminum foil and cut several slits. Spread okra and onion mixture over the grill. Stir and cook 4 to 5 minutes until slightly browned, and pods are crisp-tender. Remove to warmed bowl. Adjust seasonings and serve immediately, adding a little more lemon juice for zing. 142 calories per serving. Serves 6 to 8.

Protein 2.85   Carbohydrate 14.3   Fat 9.8   Cholesterol 0

Southern Oven Brisket

꧁꧂

8 pound brisket, trimmed of excess fat
1 generous tablespoon minced garlic
1 tablespoon celery seeds
1 tablespoon cracked white peppercorns
1 tablespoon cracked red peppercorns
1 tablespoon cracked black peppercorns
1 tablespoon ground fresh ginger
5 bay leaves, crumbled

Tomato Sauce
12 ounces tomato paste
1 cup soy sauce
½ cup Worcestershire sauce
1 cup molasses
1 tablespoon Louisiana hot sauce
2 yellow onions, thinly sliced
 Red wine

Preheat oven to 350 degrees. Tear off 2 pieces of aluminum foil, large enough to completely enclose the brisket. Place the meat on the doubled sheets of foil and rub all over with garlic followed by a combination of celery seeds, pepper, ginger, and bay leaf. Mix tomato paste, soy sauce, Worcestershire sauce, molasses and hot sauce, and smear over meat. Score fat side of the brisket and place onions on top. Seal foil well and place top side up on a rack in a roasting pan. Bake for 4 hours.

Open the foil to expose the onion and cook for another hour. Remove meat to a heated plate and keep warm. Scrap loose as much of the sauce as possible, avoiding blackened parts, degrease, and place in a saucepan with a small portion of red wine. Simmer over medium heat until reduced by half. Slice brisket thinly against the grain and serve with heated sauce. 1282 calories per serving. Serves 6 to 8 generously.

Protein 139   Carbohydrate 44   Fat 59   Cholesterol 421

Summer Lime Pie

Crust
1	cup fine graham cracker crumbs
½	cup pecans, toasted
½	cup sugar
½	cup butter, melted

Preheat oven to 375 degrees. Bake pecans on a cookie sheet until golden brown but not overcooked. Cool, and whir in food processor until as fine as the graham crackers. Add pecans and sugar to crumbs and combine. Stir in melted butter and mix well. Use your fingers to firmly pat into a 9 inch pie pan. Chill in refrigerator until firm, or bake for 8 minutes and chill.

Filling
4	large eggs
1	cup sugar
	Dash of salt
¼	cup water
½	cup lime juice, freshly squeezed
1	tablespoon gelatin
1	teaspoon lime zest, no pith

Separate the eggs and place the yolks, ½ cup sugar, salt, water, and lime juice in a non-reactive saucepan and mix with beater until well blended. Sprinkle gelatin over mixture and let soften, then combine. Cook and stir over low heat until the gelatin dissolves, about 5 minutes. Chill until mixture begins to thicken. Stir in lime zest. Meanwhile, beat the egg whites until foamy and gradually add remaining sugar. Beat until stiff. Fold in the gelatin mixture and spoon into pie shell. Chill. 447 calories per serving. Serves 8.

Protein 5.5   Carbohydrates 52   Fat 25   Cholesterol 170

Summer Lime Pie.

Cocktail party food displayed on Mansion dining table.

cocktail party

Jalapeño Spiced Brochettes
Smoked Beef Tarts
Roquefort Biscuits
Dip a la Poisson

Jalapeño Spiced Brochettes.

Jalapeño Spiced Brochettes

Very spicy!

48	8 inch wooden skewers
1	clove garlic, minced and mashed
1	teaspoon salt
2	tablespoons olive oil
4	jalapeño peppers, whole and drained
96	small shrimp, shelled, deveined, and drained well

In a shallow dish, cover the skewers with water and soak for 1 hour. Make a paste of the garlic and salt. Wearing rubber gloves, slit open, de-seed, and finely chop the jalapeño. Combine garlic paste, oil, jalapeño, and shrimp. Toss until coated and marinate for 30 minutes.

Thread two shrimp onto each skewer. Grill the brochettes on a rack 4 inches over glowing coals, turning them once, for 2 or 3 minutes, or until the shrimp are pink and just firm. Or, broil on racks in a jelly roll pan under a preheated broiler until pink and firm. 36 calories per serving. Makes 48.

Protein 5.8	Carbohydrate .36	Fat 1.1	Cholesterol 43

Smoked Beef Tarts

2	packages prepared pie dough, thawed
4	teaspoons dried mustard
4	teaspoons flour
14	ounces artichoke hearts, drained
¼	pound smoked beef, thinly sliced
2	tablespoons sour cream
2	teaspoons chopped fresh dill
2	tablespoons grated Parmesan cheese
	Salt and pepper to taste
1	red bell pepper, cored, seeded, and cut into thin strips

Heat oven to 400 degrees. Combine mustard and flour, and flour both sides of pie dough. Spray 12 mini-muffin tins with a baking spray. Roll dough out; cut into rounds. Fit into pans and press into shape. Prick pastry shells and fill with pie weights. Bake 10 to 15 minutes. Cool on racks.

Rinse artichoke hearts well in cold water. Drain, pat dry, and cut into quarters. Cut beef slices into strips and roll each into a cylinder. Stir together sour cream, dill, Parmesan cheese, salt, and pepper. To assemble, spoon a little of the mixture into each shell. Top with artichokes and beef. Cut each red pepper strip in half crosswise and add to the tarts. 181 calories per serving. Makes 12 to 16.

Protein 5.1	Carbohydrate 17	Fat 10.3	Cholesterol 6.9

Roquefort Biscuits

Wonderful as an appetizer or served with a salad.

1	cup self rising flour
½	cup firm butter
2	ounces crumbled Roquefort cheese
½	cup grated Cheddar cheese
½	cup sesame seeds, toasted

Sift flour into a bowl. Using a pastry blender or 2 knives, cut in butter until mixture resembles coarse crumbs. Add Roquefort and Cheddar cheeses. With your fingers, thoroughly mix ingredients to form a dough. Cover and refrigerate.

Preheat oven to 400 degrees. Grease 2 baking sheets. Shape chilled dough into 36 balls. Toss each ball in seeds, coating well. Put balls on baking sheets and press with a fork. Bake 10 minutes or until golden around edges. Cool on racks and store in an airtight container. 58 calories per serving. Yields 36 biscuits.

Protein 1.22	Carbohydrate 2.8	Fat 4.7	Cholesterol 11.2

Dip a la Poisson

12 ounces tuna steak, grilled and cubed
8 ounces olives, pitted, drained, quartered
3 tablespoons anchovy paste
½ cup capers
6 eggs, hard cooked, shelled, and quartered
2 cloves garlic, minced
¼ cup lemon juice
½ cup olive oil
Salt and coarsely ground pepper

In a food processor, combine grilled tuna, ripe olives, anchovies, and capers. With several on and off bursts, process until ingredients are coarsely chopped. Add eggs and garlic to processor and whir again until coarsely chopped. Add lemon juice and olive oil. Blend till smooth. Season to taste with salt and coarsely ground pepper. Serve with a selection of fresh and cooled steamed vegetables. 191 calories per serving. Makes approximately 4 cups.

Protein 9.3   Carbohydrate 1.42   Fat 16.5   Cholesterol 114

Reception for Governor's Health Care Commission.

67

ann bartlett burke's italian dinner

Gnocchi di Patate
Paella alla Romano
Nutmeg Feather Cake
Seven Minute Seafoam Icing

Ann Bartlett Burke, wife of Dewey Bartlett, Oklahoma Governor from 1967 to 1971, was warmly received by one day's breakfast guests.

At that time, the third floor and the basement were unfurnished. We only entertained on the third floor occasionally because everything — chairs, cloths, china, silver, and food — had to be carried up. On the first floor we could seat thirty-six by using the dining room, sun room, living room, hall and what was called the music room, but was used as Dewey's office.

Once when there was an early morning meeting of all the state university and college presidents, we had the meeting on the third floor. I ran up to check on the arrangements thinking that I was too early for anyone to arrive. As I came down the stairs I was just in time to greet them as they all came up the stairs. They were all too polite to comment on my curlers and slippers.

When serving a sit down dinner for eighty-five to ninety guests, the third floor ballroom is used.

The Governor and Mrs. Dewey Bartlett greet guests during the 1967 Inaugural Ball.

Ann Bartlett Burke, former First Lady, is grateful to Wilhelmina Cooper, "a really fine cook," for this favorite dinner. Entertaining was arranged around the days Wilhelmina was at the Mansion. These dishes were served with Veal Scaloppine. Cheese and fruit with coffee rounded out the meal.

Gnocchi di Patate

3	tablespoons olive oil
¾	cup chopped onions
½	cup chopped celery
1	tablespoon minced parsley
1	clove garlic, minced
18	ounces Italian tomatoes
4	ounces tomato paste
1	teaspoon salt
½	teaspoon pepper
½	teaspoon basil
½	teaspoon oregano
1	bay leaf

In oil, sauté the onions, celery, parsley, and garlic. Add tomatoes, paste, salt, and pepper. Boil and cook over low heat 45 minutes. Add basil, oregano, and bay leaf. Cook 15 minutes; discard bay leaf.

Dumplings

3	potatoes
4	cups flour
6	quarts water
1	tablespoon salt
	Parmesan cheese, grated

Cook potatoes and mash. Place on floured surface and mix with flour. Knead and roll into finger thin strips; cut into 2 inch strips. Boil water and salt. Cook 20 gnocchi at a time until they rise; remove, drain, and put in serving dish. Cover with tomato sauce to keep dumplings moist. When gnocchi are cooked, add rest of sauce; top with cheese. 80 calories per serving. Makes 40 to 60 dumplings.

Protein 1.94   Carbohydrate 14.3   Fat 1.57   Cholesterol .172

Paella alla Romano

½	pound butter
¾	cup sliced onions
3	packages frozen peas
	Salt and pepper to taste
¼	cup water
¼	pound prosciutto ham, cut into strips
½	teaspoon sugar

Melt butter, brown onions. Add peas, salt, pepper, and water. Cover and cook 10 minutes. Add ham and cook another 10 minutes; sprinkle with sugar and toss. 199 calories per serving. Serves 8.

Protein 5   Carbohydrate 6.2   Fat 17.7   Cholesterol 53

Nutmeg Feather Cake

This is a recipe of Mrs. Burke's sister.

⅓	cup butter
¼	cup shortening
1½	cups sugar
2	eggs, beaten
2	cups flour
1	teaspoon baking powder
1	teaspoon soda
1	teaspoon cinnamon
½	teaspoon nutmeg
½	teaspoon allspice
1	cup buttermilk
½	teaspoon vanilla

Preheat oven to 350 degrees. Cream butter, shortening, and sugar. Add eggs and beat. Blend in sifted dry ingredients alternately with buttermilk and vanilla. Bake in 2 greased 9 inch pans 25 minutes. 227 calories per serving. Serves 8.

Protein 3.76   Carbohydrate 28   Fat 11.1   Cholesterol 61

Seven Minute Seafoam Icing

2 unbroken egg whites
1½ cups sugar
5 tablespoons cold water
¼ teaspoon cream of tartar
1½ tablespoons corn syrup
4 tablespoons caramelized sugar
1 teaspoon vanilla

Place unbroken egg whites, sugar, cold water, cream of tartar, and corn syrup over rapidly boiling water. Beat constantly with a rotary beater for seven minutes. Add caramelized sugar and vanilla and continue to beat until icing becomes the right consistency for spreading. To make caramelized sugar, place 1 cup sugar in a heavy skillet over medium heat, and stir until it dissolves. Continue stirring until the sugar is smooth and turns into a light shade of caramel.

Flavored vinegar, bottled by Mansion Administrator Steven Bunch, in Mrs. Walters' antique decantors.

Displayed on the antique game table in the Mansion Library are the Spinach Salad and Strawberries with Raspberry Vinaigrette, Boiled Brisket with Horseradish Sauce, Green Bean and Potato Mash, and Doretha's Strawberry Pie.

dinner party

Spinach Salad and Strawberries
with Raspberry Vinaigrette
Boiled Brisket with Horseradish Sauce
Green Bean and Potato Mash
Doretha's Strawberry Pie

Invitation for a reception at the White House from President
Roosevelt to Governor Frantz on February 1, 1906.

Spinach Salad and Strawberries with Raspberry Vinaigrette

10 ounces fresh spinach, washed and ribbed
1 pint fresh strawberries, hulled and thinly sliced lengthwise
Sesame seeds

Dressing
¼ cup raspberries, fresh or thawed
¼ cup raspberry vinegar
1 tablespoon vinegar
½ cup canola or lite vegetable oil
Sugar to taste
Sesame seeds

To prepare dressing, mash berries well and combine with vinegar, paprika, and oil. Add sugar until dressing is lightly sweetened. Place spinach in a large bowl and add a light coat of dressing. Divide among six chilled salad plates; mix in sliced berries and sprinkle lightly with sesame seeds. 202 calories per serving. Serves 6.

Protein 2.1   Carbohydrate 9.4   Fat 18.7   Cholesterol 0

Boiled Brisket with Horseradish Sauce

This is an unusual variation of an Oklahoma favorite. A pot roast could probably be prepared this way, also.

6 pound brisket, well trimmed of excess fat
1 large oven cooking bag
1 tablespoon flour
4 medium onions, quartered
2 tablespoons salt
4 bay leaves
2 teaspoons crushed dried thyme
6 celery stalks, cut in half

Preheat oven to 300 degrees. Put flour in cooking bag, twist shut, and shake to coat bag. Put meat in the cooking bag and place in roasting pan. Add all other ingredients to bag plus 2 to 3 cups of water. Tie bag shut and bake 3 to 4 hours. Brisket should be tender but not falling apart. Remove from oven and let rest in its juice until ready to serve.

Horseradish Sauce — *the secret of this super brisket!*
½ stick butter
2 cups chicken stock, heated
1 cup diced onion
2 tablespoons flour
1 tablespoon plus 1 teaspoon fresh lemon juice
1 teaspoon white pepper
5 tablespoons prepared horseradish
Salt to taste

In a saucepan, add diced onions to melted butter and brown lightly. Sprinkle in the flour, mix well, and add the hot stock. Stir and simmer for a few minutes until thickened. Mix in the lemon juice and pepper; simmer for 10 minutes stirring occasionally. Add the horseradish and salt. 928 calories per serving. Serves 8.

Protein 103   Carbohydrate 10.3   Fat 51   Cholesterol 333

Green Beans and Potato Mash

❧

*"This may sound weird, but it is soooo good," says
Steven Bunch, Mansion administrator.*

1	pound baking potatoes, not new potatoes, cubed
1	pound fresh green beans, snapped
5-6	tablespoons butter
½	teaspoon crushed rosemary
½	teaspoon ground nutmeg, or to taste
	Salt and pepper to taste

Preheat oven to 450 degrees. In a saucepan, cover
potatoes with water; bring to a boil and add the
green beans. Cook for 12 to 15 minutes until the
beans are just tender. Do not overcook. Drain and
puree in a food processor, scrapping the sides
frequently to mix well.

Cut butter into small pieces; add to mixture along
with rosemary, nutmeg, salt, and pepper. Pour into
an oven proof serving dish and top with a small
chunk of butter. Bake for 20 minutes and serve
immediately. 151 calories per serving. Serves 8.

Protein 2.1   Carbohydrate 19.3   Fat 7.9   Cholesterol 20.6

Doretha's Strawberry Pie

❧

*Doretha Hayes has worked at the Mansion for 17
years. I remember enjoying this delicious dessert the
first time I was at the Mansion during
Governor David Boren's term.*

Crust
1½	cups flour
½	cup oil
2	tablespoons milk
2	teaspoons sugar
1	teaspoon salt

Preheat oven to 375 degrees. Combine ingredients
and pat into pie shell. Bake for 15 minutes.

Pie Filling
1	cup sugar
2	tablespoons cornstarch
1	cup water
3	tablespoons strawberry Jell-O® granules
1	quart strawberries
1	tablespoon vanilla
	Whipped cream

Mix sugar, cornstarch, and water together. Cook
over moderate heat until mixture comes to a boil,
simmer until thick. Remove from heat; add
Jell-O® and stir well. Allow to cool. Fold in
strawberries and vanilla, and pour into shell. Right
before serving, top with whipped cream. 262
calories per serving. Serves 8.

Protein .67   Carbohydrate 34.6   Fat 14   Cholesterol .52

Platinum watches were given to the Bartletts by King Faisal of Saudi Arabia during visit to Saudi Arabia in January 1974. These earrings and cufflinks were worn by Governor and Mrs. Walters at their Inaugural Ball, 1991.

a state dinner in oklahoma

Onion Soup with Mushrooms
Mustard Herb Crusted Rack of Lamb
with Cilantro Mint Sauce
Garlic Herb Roasted New Potatoes
Asparagus with Horseradish Dill Sauce
Fabulous Dessert

Fabulous Dessert.

Onion Soup with Mushrooms

8   tablespoons butter
6   onions, thinly sliced
2   teaspoons dried thyme
8   cups chicken stock
3   tablespoons reduced sodium soy sauce
6   ounces shiitake or chanterelle
     mushrooms, trimmed, thinly sliced
2   scallions, sliced
     Salt and pepper

In a large pot, melt 4 tablespoons butter and add onions, salt, and thyme. Cook over medium heat, stirring frequently, until onions are golden but not scorched, about 20 minutes. The slower onions cook, the more mellow the flavor. Add and bring chicken stock to a simmer; cook covered for 30 minutes. Season to taste with soy sauce, salt, and pepper. Strain soup and discard the onions. Recipe can be made several days ahead up to this point. Cover and refrigerate.

Before serving, reheat soup in large pot. In a skillet, melt the remaining 4 tablespoons butter and sauté mushrooms until just softened, about 4 minutes. Divide mushrooms equally among warmed soup bowls and ladle onion soup on top. Garnish with sliced scallion tops. Serve at once. 244 calories per serving. Serves 6.

Protein 9.3   Carbohydrate 11.6   Fat 18.4   Cholesterol 45

Mustard Herb Crusted Rack of Lamb with Cilantro Mint Sauce

8   ounces Dijon mustard
2   tablespoons garlic paste
1   tablespoon coarse ground pepper
8   ounces herb seasoned stuffing mix
     Rack of lamb, trimmed and frenched

Preheat oven to 350 degrees. Prepare a paste of mustard, garlic paste, and pepper; coat lamb. Pour dry herb seasoned mixture into a bowl large enough to accommodate the lamb and press mixture onto lamb. Spray a roasting pan with non-stick coating and place rack in pan with ribs intertwined. Roast for 30 minutes or until internal temperature reaches 140 degrees. Remove from oven and cool for 5 minutes before carving.

Cilantro Mint Sauce

1   cup packed, chopped fresh cilantro
½   cup packed, chopped fresh mint leaves,
1   teaspoon finely chopped and seeded fresh
     jalapeño pepper, or to taste
1   small clove garlic
1   teaspoon grated gingerroot
2   tablespoons fresh lemon juice
¼   teaspoon ground cumin
1   tablespoon mint jelly
     Salt and pepper to taste
¼   cup plain yogurt

Puree all the ingredients except the yogurt, scraping the sides to mix well. Transfer mixture to a bowl and whisk in the yogurt. Entire entrée has 479 calories per serving. Makes about 1 cup.

Protein 29   Carbohydrate 27   Fat 28.5   Cholesterol 96

Garlic Herb Roasted New Potatoes

2   pounds new potatoes, scrubbed
     and halved
1   stick butter, melted and cooled
¼   cup chopped fresh parsley
1   tablespoon chopped garlic
2   lemons, rind grated
     Salt and pepper to taste

Place prepared potatoes in pot and cover with water. Bring to a boil; lower heat and simmer until potatoes start to soften, about 10 minutes. Drain potatoes and place on cookie sheet or jelly roll pan. Mix butter, parsley, garlic, and grated lemon zest. Pour over potatoes and toss well to coat. Place pan approximately 4 inches under broiler and cook until browned, stir until well browned all over. Season with salt and pepper. 475 calories per serving. Serves 4 to 6.

| Protein 7.3 | Carbohydrate 77 | Fat 16.7 | Cholesterol 44 |

Asparagus with Horseradish Dill Sauce

1½	pounds fresh asparagus, washed and trimmed
10½	ounces chicken broth
½	cup fat free mayonnaise
3	tablespoons plain yogurt
2	tablespoons finely chopped dill pickle
2	tablespoons fresh chopped dill
4	ounces prepared horseradish

Place asparagus in a glass dish with chicken broth. Cover with plastic wrap and microwave until just crisp tender, 8 to 10 minutes. Mix the mayonnaise, yogurt, chopped pickle, and dill until smooth. Add horseradish, a tablespoon at a time, until it is forceful but not overpowering. Drain asparagus and place in warm serving dish. Serve with sauce either covering asparagus, or as an accompaniment. 72 calories per serving. Serves 6.

| Protein 4.2 | Carbohydrate 7.2 | Fat .58 | Cholesterol .21 |

Fabulous Dessert

Since we entertain so much, I wanted a pretty no-fat or low-fat dessert. Administrator Steven Bunch created this recipe which always receives "raves" when served!

	Angel food cake mix, white or lemon
1	pint plain yogurt
3	tablespoons cinnamon
1	tablespoon vanilla extract
¼	cup honey or to taste
6	passion fruit, pulp removed
6	tablespoons sugar
¼	cup water
1	cup thinly sliced strawberries
6	kiwi, peeled and thinly sliced
1	cup thinly sliced and seeded kumquats
3-6	blood oranges, depending on size, peeled, sliced, and seeded
	Fresh blackberries, blueberries, raspberries, sliced mangos, or sliced peaches

Prepare cake according to directions. In a small bowl, combine the yogurt and vanilla, and enough honey to make the sauce sweet. Cover and refrigerate. Place passion fruit, sugar, and water in a small saucepan. Bring to boil, lower to simmer, and cook until sauce reaches a syrup consistency. Pour into small bowl, cover and chill.

When ready to serve, thinly slice the cake. Place 2 to 3 tablespoons honey-yogurt sauce on a dessert plate; tilt plate to spread. Fan out 3 slices of cake and, starting in the middle and working to one side, lay out the kiwi, strawberries, and berries, finishing with the kumquats. Spoon the passion fruit on top. 560 calories per serving. Serves 6.

| Protein 14.2 | Carbohydrate 126 | Fat 2.2 | Cholesterol 4.7 |

This menu was served to Governor Walters' Cabinet at a dinner in honor of new cabinet member, Secretary of Policy and Management Jerry Goodman.

governor's cabinet dinner

Grilled Veal Chops with Rosemary
Melon Seed Pasta
with Dried Cherries and Almonds
Summer Squash and Onions
Lemon Mousse with Blackberries

Grilled Veal Chops with Rosemary.

Grilled Veal Chops with Rosemary

〰

2 tablespoons freshly grated lemon zest
2 tablespoons minced fresh rosemary
3 tablespoons fresh lemon juice
⅓ cup olive oil
 Salt and pepper to taste
4 1¼ inch thick loin veal chops, boned,
 leave tails attached

In a large shallow dish, make a marinade of 1½ tablespoons zest, 1½ tablespoons minced rosemary, lemon juice, oil, salt, and pepper. Combine well. Sprinkle tail of each chop with remaining zest and rosemary. Wrap each tail flush against the loin portion of each chop; skewer with a wooden pick. Add the chops to the marinade, cover and chill, turning several times. Grill the chops on a rack over glowing coals for 7 minutes on each side for medium rare. 538 calories per serving. Serves 4.

Protein 46   Carbohydrate .94   Fat 37.5   Cholesterol 168

Melon Seed Pasta
with Dried Cherries and Almonds

〰

Orzo can be used instead of melon seed.

2 cans prepared chicken stock
1 teaspoon ground turmeric
1 cup Melon Seed pasta
1 tablespoon freshly grated orange zest
3 tablespoons orange juice concentrate
3 tablespoons olive oil
⅓ cup dried cherries or raisins
3 tablespoons slivered and toasted almonds
3 tablespoons chives, cut in ½ inch pieces

In a saucepan, bring to a boil the chicken stock and enough water to make six cups. Add the turmeric and pasta and boil 6 to 8 minutes until al dente.

Drain pasta and refresh under cold water. Blend the zest, orange juice concentrate, and olive oil until emulsified. In a large bowl, toss the well drained pasta with the dressing, add the cherries, almonds, and chives. Serve at room temperature. 287 calories per serving. Serves 4 to 6.

Protein 8.8   Carbohydrate 36.6   Fat 12   Cholesterol .42

Summer Squash and Onions

〰

4 tablespoons unsalted butter
4 cups coarsely chopped onions
1 pound medium yellow squash, sliced
1 pound medium zucchini, sliced
 Sugar to taste
 Salt and red pepper to taste
¼ cup chicken broth

Melt butter in a medium saucepan over low heat. Add onions and cook, covered, for 20 minutes. Add squash, zucchini, sugar, salt, pepper, and broth. Cook for 45 minutes, stirring often, until squash and onions are very tender. Remove from liquid with slotted spoon and serve hot. 110 calories per serving. Serves 6.

Protein 2.37   Carbohydrate 10.4   Fat 8.6   Cholesterol 22

Lemon Mousse with Blackberries

〰

Very pretty dessert — great for a ladies luncheon.

1 large lemon
1 cup fresh blackberries
1¼ ounce package gelatin
¼ cup water
3 eggs at room temperature
¾ cup sugar
1½ cups chilled heavy cream
 Fresh mint

Using fine grater, remove zest from lemon. Juice the lemons; pour over zest. Sprinkle the gelatin over the water in a small saucepan and set aside.

In another bowl, beat the eggs, gradually add the sugar and continue beating until mixture is light yellow and fluffy. Stir in lemon juice and zest. Completely dissolve the gelatin over medium heat.

With mixer on slow speed, combine gelatin and egg mixtures to form a mousse. In another bowl, whip 1 cup cream until stiff peaks form and fold into the mousse with a spatula. Set this bowl into a larger bowl of ice water; stir to the point of thickening. Fold in all but 8 berries. Quickly distribute the mixture into dessert dishes or champagne glasses. Cover and chill for 3 hours.

Just before serving, whip the remaining cream. Place a dollop on each serving and garnish with the remaining blackberries and a sprig of fresh mint. 441 calories per serving. Serves 6 to 8.

Protein 6.5   Carbohydrate 49   Fat 25   Cholesterol 22

Buffalo, by United Designs of Noble, Oklahoma, along with handmade Indian print bag, was presented to the nation's governors, inviting them to Oklahoma for the National Governors Association Conference in Tulsa, Oklahoma, held in August of 1993. Certificate admitting William H. Murray to practice in the United States Court, Southern District of Indian Territory, at Ardmore, on April 18, 1898.

Holiday dinner menu displayed on buffet.

holiday dinner

*A Salad of Mixed Greens with Citrus
and Herbed Blueberry Vinaigrette
Lobster Cakes with Tomato Butter Sauce
Oven Roasted Lamb Shanks
Garlic Mashed Potatoes
Sinful Bread Pudding
with Caramel Sauce*

Steven Bunch, Mansion Administrator, remembers Shirley Bellmon's expertise in the kitchen.

Shirley Bellmon lived with her husband, Henry, in the Oklahoma Governor's Mansion from 1963 to 1967 and 1987 to 1991. She was always at home in the kitchen, one of her true loves. An avid gardener as well, the former First Lady canned many fruits and vegetables from the Bellmon farm. Canned apple butter and fresh peach preserves lined the Mansion pantry shelves. Revered for her homemade pies, she once prepared dessert for a series of dinners. Mrs. Bellmon baked for several days filling the pantry with 25 delicious pecan pies.

Former Governor Henry Bellmon, who served from 1987 to 1991, and his wife, Shirley, with Steven Bunch, Mansion Administrator.

Salad of Mixed Greens with Citrus and Herbed Blueberry Vinaigrette

❧

6	cups mixed greens, torn
⅔	cup herbed blueberry vinaigrette
2	large ruby grapefruit, or 4 seedless oranges, peeled and sectioned
⅔	cup croutons

In a large bowl, combine the greens and vinaigrette; toss lightly to mix. When ready to serve, divide among 6 plates and top with citrus sections and croutons.

Vinaigrette

⅔	cup blueberries, fresh or frozen
¼	cup white wine vinegar
½	cup balsamic vinegar
1	tablespoon sugar
	Salt and pepper to taste
4	tablespoons salad oil
½	cup dry basil, crushed

In a food processor, combine blueberries, vinegars, sugar, pepper and salt. Process until smooth. Strain mixture through a sieve to remove skins. In a screw top jar, combine the blueberry mixture with salad oil and basil. Cover and shake well. Chill for at least one hour and lightly coat salad. 149 calories per serving. Serves 6.

Protein 2.17	Carbohydrate 15.6	Fat 9.3	Cholesterol 0

Lobster Cakes with Tomato Butter Sauce

❧

½	cup whipping cream
4	slices white bread, crusts trimmed
2	eggs, beaten
2	tablespoons fresh lemon juice
12	ounces cooked lobster meat, or one 3 pound lobster, cleaned, cooked, shelled and diced. If possible, use lobster tails, which have a much better flavor. Salt and pepper to taste
1	tablespoon oil
1	tablespoon butter

In a small saucepan, cook the cream over medium heat, stirring occasionally until reduced by half. Cool. Make crumbs of bread with food processor. Combine the cream, bread crumbs, eggs, lemon juice, lobster, salt, and pepper in a large bowl. Shape into ⅓ cup patties. Can be prepared 24 hours in advance; store covered in the refrigerator.

Preheat oven to 400 degrees. In a skillet, sauté the lobster patties until golden brown in the melted butter and oil. Drain on a cookie sheet, layered with paper towels, for several minutes. Remove towels and bake in oven for 5 to 7 minutes.

Tomato Butter Sauce

7	Italian tomatoes, seeded and chopped
2	bay leaves
½	teaspoon white pepper
½	shallot, diced
1	cup dry white wine
½	cup green onion tops, thinly sliced
4	sticks chilled butter, not margarine, cut into tablespoons

Puree the tomatoes in a food processor. In a large saucepan, cook the puree, bay leaves, white pepper, shallot, and white wine over medium-high heat until the mixture is reduced by three-quarters.

Remove from heat; add butter, a tablespoon at a time, whisking constantly.

Strain through a sieve and return to the saucepan. Keep sauce warm over low heat until serving. Pour one-fourth cup of tomato butter sauce on each plate, top with a lobster cake, and garnish with green onions. 840 calories per serving. Serves 6.

Protein 17.6   Carbohydrate 17   Fat 77   Cholesterol 331

Oven Roasted Lamb Shanks

❧

6	one pound lamb shanks
	Salt and pepper to taste
2	cups all purpose flour
½	cup olive oil
1	onion, diced
1	carrot, peeled and diced
2	celery stalks, diced
½	fennel bulb, sliced
2	cups dry white wine
7	tablespoons Dijon mustard
2	bay leaves
1	tablespoon dried basil, crushed
2	garlic bulbs, cut in half
6	cups chicken broth

Preheat oven to 350 degrees. Sprinkle the lamb shanks with salt and pepper and dredge them in flour. In a skillet, heat half the olive oil and sear the shanks 2 or 3 at a time until golden brown, adding oil as necessary. Transfer shanks to a heavy oven proof casserole dish with a lid.

In the frying skillet and juices, sauté the onion, carrot, celery, and fennel until tender. Add the remaining flour and continue cooking until the vegetables turn golden brown. Add the white wine and boil to reduce the mixture by half, then add the mustard, bay leaf, basil, garlic and broth, and bring to a boil.

Pour the vegetable mixture over the shanks, and bake for 2 hours, or until very tender, turning the shanks every 20 minutes. Remove the shanks from the pan and strain liquid through a sieve, pressing the vegetables through with the back of a spoon.

Cook the liquid in a saucepan over medium heat until thick enough to coat a spoon. Add salt and pepper as needed, and skim off the fat with a spoon. Slice the meat from the lamb shanks and serve on a warmed platter with sauce. 1390 calories per serving. Serves 6.

Protein 148   Carbohydrate 39   Fat 62   Cholesterol 300

Garlic Mashed Potatoes

❧

7	garlic cloves, unpeeled
5	russet potatoes, scrubbed and quartered
1	cup heavy cream
1	stick butter
	Salt and white pepper to taste

Bake garlic cloves in a 300 degree oven for 45 minutes, set aside. Place the potatoes in a large pot and add water to cover. Bring to a boil, reduce heat, and simmer until tender, about 15 minutes; drain. Cut off the ends of the roasted garlic cloves and squeeze pulp into another saucepan. Add cream and butter; heat until the butter is melted. Set aside and keep warm.

Place the potatoes in a food mill or potato ricer held over a large bowl and puree, or mash potatoes in a large bowl with a mixer. Stir in the warm cream mixture and blend until the right consistency. Add salt and pepper. Serve immediately, or cover with foil and place in warm oven for up to 20 minutes before serving. 384 calories per serving. Serves 6.

Protein 3.1   Carbohydrate 24.7   Fat 31.3   Cholesterol 100

Sinful Bread Pudding with Caramel Sauce

❧

1   baguette, a loaf of true French bread, sliced into rounds
1   stick butter, melted
1   teaspoon nutmeg
1½   cups sugar
¾   cup all purpose flour
9   eggs
6   cups heavy cream, or 1½ quarts
       Sifted powdered sugar for sprinkling

Preheat oven to 300 degrees. Place the bread rounds on a baking sheet. Brush one side with butter and bake until golden brown, 10 minutes. In a large bowl, combine the nutmeg, sugar, and flour. Whisk in the eggs and cream until smooth.

In an 11 inch spring-form pan, layer the bread slices buttered side up. Pour the egg mixture over the bread slices and let sit for 20 minutes. Cover the pan with aluminum foil. Place the pan in a larger baking pan, add hot water halfway up the sides of the pan, and bake 1 hour.

Remove the foil and bake another hour; remove from the water bath and let cool. Serve on a pool of the caramel sauce and top with powdered sugar.

Caramel Sauce

1   teaspoon fresh lemon juice
1½   cups sugar
⅓   cup water
1   cup heavy cream
3   tablespoons butter

In a saucepan, bring the juice, sugar, and water to a boil, stirring to dissolve the sugar. Cook over a low heat and watch carefully to avoid burning.

When syrup becomes golden brown, remove from heat. Slowly stir the cream into the syrup, blend in the butter, and stir until a smooth consistency is reached. Set aside and keep warm. 1227 calories per serving. Serves 8 to 10.

Protein 14.4   Carbohydrate 66   Fat 102   Cholesterol 648

The First Lady's office and the adjoining family room of the Governor's Mansion were remodeled in 1991 to form one open room. This new spacious environment allows Mrs. Walters to accommodate both her work and family needs.

This menu was served by Linda Trippe Catering for a cocktail party at the Mansion.

a catered evening

Brie Baked in Puff Pastry
Breadsticks with Aioli
Pesto Tart
Spinach Mushroom Paté
Sausage Pistachio Paté
Linda's Brownies
Chocolate Chip Walnut Cookies

Breadsticks with Aioli.

Brie Baked in Puff Pastry

A quick, easy, and delicious appetizer.

1 Wheel of brie cheese
1 Large puff pastry dough
   Preserves, optional

Roll out a large square of puff pastry dough and thin with a rolling pin. Place the brie on the puff pastry dough, and spread with a thin layer of preserves. Gather edges of the dough to the center of the brie and form a knot to seal edges.

Bake in 400 degree oven for 5 to 7 minutes; don't melt the brie too much. Serve with fresh fruit and crackers. 336 calories per serving. Serves 12.

Protein 8   Carbohydrate 30   Fat 17.2   Cholesterol 68

This bronze Remington Statue, entitled Will Rogers Equestrian, was presented to Governor Walters during the opening week of the Will Rogers Follies in New York City on May 4, 1991.

Breadsticks with Aioli

1   tablespoon dry yeast
1   cup warm water
1   cup milk
2   tablespoons sugar
¼   cup cornmeal
3   tablespoons olive oil
⅔   cup finely chopped onion
2   tablespoons rosemary
2   teaspoons salt
1   tablespoon cracked black pepper
2   cups whole wheat flour
4   cups all purpose flour

In a large bowl, mix the yeast and the warm water together. After 5 minutes, add the milk and sugar. If using a mixer, be sure to use a breadhook. If using your hands, use a heavy wooden spoon and keep mixing. Add cornmeal, olive oil, onion, rosemary, salt, and pepper. Then add whole wheat flour and combine thoroughly. Add all purpose flour one cup at a time using only 3 cups.

Place last cup of flour on counter, add dough and knead, adding flour until dough is no longer sticky. Knead dough with both hands. Fold dough in half, turn one-fourth turn and push; repeat for 5 minutes. Place dough in bowl, cover with plastic; let sit in warm place until doubled in size. Repeat.

Preheat oven to 300 degrees. Roll dough into large rectangle ¼ inch thick. Cut into 10 inch strips, ½ inch wide. Dust baking sheet with cornmeal, add breadsticks, and twist. Bake 25 minutes. Breadsticks should be quite dry. Yields 25 breadsticks.

Aioli

2   large eggs
2   cups lite olive oil
4   cloves garlic, peeled and finely chopped
     Salt and pepper

Beat eggs with a whisk. Add the olive oil, in a tiny stream, very slowly. The mixture will emulsify and begin to look like mayonnaise. Add all the oil, then garlic, salt, and pepper to taste. When served as dip with breadsticks, 238 calories per serving.

Protein 3.8   Carbohydrate 20   Fat 16   Cholesterol 22.6

Pesto Torte

20   ounces cream cheese
4   ounces sour cream
2   cups minced fresh basil leaves
¼   cup olive oil
3   cloves garlic, peeled
      Salt and pepper to taste

Using a mixer, whip the cream cheese and sour cream together until smooth. In a food processor, puree basil leaves, olive oil, and garlic. Season to taste with salt and pepper.

Place one-third of the cream cheese mixture in a quart bowl lined with plastic wrap. Pat flat and cover with one-half of the pesto, spreading to the edges so the green is visible. Repeat ending with layer of cream cheese.

Chill for 2 to 3 hours. To serve, invert bowl on plate. Remove bowl and plastic. Serve with crackers. 126 calories per serving. Serves 24.

Protein 2.7   Carbohydrate 4.7   Fat 12   Cholesterol 26.7

Pesto Torte.

Spinach Mushroom Paté

4   tablespoons olive oil
1   medium white onion, chopped
15   ounces mushrooms, thinly sliced
1   pound fresh spinach, destemmed, washed, and lightly chopped
3   large eggs
     Salt and pepper to taste

Preheat oven to 275 degrees. In a large skillet, sauté the onion in the olive oil. When barely transparent, add the mushrooms and cook until only a small amount of liquid remains. Add spinach which will wilt very quickly. Let mixture cool. Beat in eggs, season with salt and pepper. Place in 5 by 9 inch pan lined with enough plastic wrap to cover the top. Bake in a water bath for 45 to 60 minutes. Chill overnight. 35.6 calories per serving. Serves 32.

Protein 1.9   Carbohydrate 2.3   Fat 2.47   Cholesterol 25.7

Sausage Pistachio Paté

2   tablespoons olive oil
1   yellow onion, chopped
2   cloves garlic, minced
20   ounces pork sausage
3   large eggs
½   cup shelled and toasted, unsalted pistachio nuts
1   tablespoon fennel seeds
     Salt and pepper to taste

Preheat oven to 300 degrees. In a skillet, sauté the onion in oil. Add garlic and sausage; cook well. Drain grease; cool. Add eggs, pistachio nuts, and fennel seeds. Season with salt and pepper. Place in 5 by 9 inch pan lined with plastic wrap large enough to cover the top. Bake in water bath for 45 to 55 minutes. When done, the center will be firm. Chill overnight. 55 calories per serving. Serves 24.

Protein 1.85   Carbohydrate 1.53   Fat 4.7   Cholesterol 37

Sausage Pistachio Paté and Spinach Mushroom Paté.

Linda's Brownies

1¼   pound unsalted butter
1½   cups unsweetened cocoa
4   cups sugar
¼   cup vanilla extract
8   whole eggs
2   cups flour
    Powdered sugar
    Cinnamon

Preheat oven to 300 degrees. Melt butter, sugar, and chocolate; cool slightly. Beat eggs lightly in a large mixing bowl. Stir in vanilla and very slowly, to prevent eggs from curdling, add chocolate mixture. Blend; add flour and mix. Pour into foil-lined 12 by 16 inch pan, greased and floured lightly. Bake 15 minutes. Inserted toothpick will not be clean; do not overbake. Dust with powdered sugar and cinnamon. Cut into mini-squares. 173 calories per serving. Serves 48.

Protein 2.06   Carbohydrate 21.5   Fat 10.7   Cholesterol 70

Chocolate Chip Walnut Cookies

2½   cups flour
1   teaspoon baking soda
1   teaspoon salt
½   pound unsalted butter, softened
¾   cup packed brown sugar
¾   cup granulated sugar
2   large eggs
1   teaspoon vanilla
3   cups chocolate chips
1   cup chopped walnuts

Preheat oven to 350 degrees. In a mixing bowl, combine flour, baking soda, and salt. In a larger bowl, cream the butter and two sugars. Beat in eggs and vanilla. Gradually add dry ingredients until well blended. Stir in chocolate chips and walnuts. Drop well rounded teaspoonfuls onto ungreased cookie sheets. Bake 8 to 10 minutes. 72 calories per serving. Yields 8 dozen cookies.

Protein .98   Carbohydrate 8.3   Fat 4.6   Cholesterol 11.2

Linda's Brownies and Chocolate Chip Walnut Cookies.

pizza party

Pizza

We often have Mansion Pizza Parties when entertaining friends or staff or anytime we want a fun, relaxed, casual evening.

Selecting toppings is no casual affair.

The sun room located on the first floor of the Mansion.

Pizza

1   cup water
1   package dry yeast
3   cups flour
1   teaspoon salt
3   tablespoons olive oil plus more
     for brushing
1   tablespoon honey
1   cup grated mozzarella cheese
2   pounds roma tomatoes, sliced
     Assorted pizza toppings

Pour ¼ cup water into microwave safe container and heat until just warm. Sprinkle dry yeast in water and let set until dissolved, approximately 2 minutes. Combine flour and salt in large mixing bowl. In a small bowl, combine olive oil, honey, remaining water, and yeast mixture. Pour into flour and mix thoroughly.

Place bowl in warm area, covered, and let rise for 1 hour. Dough may be made to this point and stored in refrigerator for one day, if covered well with plastic wrap. Makes dough for 4 medium pizzas. To prepare pizzas, place pizza stone on middle rack of oven, sprinkle with corn meal, and preheat oven to 375 degrees. Put dough on a floured work surface and pat out to desired thickness and size. Sprinkle pizza paddle with corn meal and slide under dough.

Lightly brush dough with olive or sesame oil and sprinkle with ½ cup mozzarella cheese. Spread roma tomatoes on top. Add additional ingredients such as red or yellow bell pepper rings, shiitake or other fresh mushroom slices, mandarin oranges, diced garlic, cracked black pepper, pineapple rings, pepperoni, thinly sliced chicken breast marinated in barbecue sauce and honey, sesame oil, fresh basil, rosemary, and minced garlic. Top with remaining mozzarella. For spicy pizza, sprinkle with hot oil.

Place pizza on stone and cook approximately 15 minutes, until bottom is golden brown. Remove from oven with pizza paddle, place on platter, and cut into individual servings. Serve with Romaine salad garnished with extra toppings from pizzas and Italian dressing.

Preparing the dough.

Chief of Staff Bill Johnson tossing pizza dough.

Elizabeth Walters, Karen and Lindsey Copeland, and Governor Walters prepare their pizza.

First Lady Rhonda Walters garnishes her personal pizza.

Kristen Walters adds a touch of garlic to her personal pizza.

Numerous toppings add variety to the pizzas.

Governor Walters cuts the finished product.

Elizabeth Walters adds her personal touch to her pizza.

family favorites

Spicy Grilled Shrimp
Creamy Corn Pudding
Lima Bean Casserole
Doris Cross' Old Fashioned Chicken and Dumplings
Casual Chicken Kiev
Oven Meatballs with Sauerbraten Sauce
Curried Orange Chicken
Cream Cheese Brownie Cake
Streusel Pecan Pie Squares
Mousse au Chocolat

The Mansion's spiral grand staircase seen from the third floor.

Spicy Grilled Shrimp

❧

3	pounds large shrimp, 10 to 12 per pound, uncooked and deveined
2	tablespoons lite soy sauce
2	tablespoons dry white wine
2	tablespoons white wine vinegar
4	tablespoons chopped garlic
4	tablespoons finely minced gingerroot
4	tablespoons sesame oil
2	tablespoons canola oil
1	tablespoon sugar
2	tablespoons ground red pepper
½	teaspoon salt
¼	cup finely chopped onion
3	tablespoons coarsely chopped chives

To butterfly shrimp, slice length of the back, about half way in. Pat dry, place sliced side down. Gently press. Shrimp tails must curl up and point forward. In a bowl, mix all the ingredients except the chives. Add the cleaned shrimp and marinade. Let marinate at least 1 hour, tossing shrimp often.

Place shrimp on heated grill in the butterfly position and cover. Cook five minutes or until the shrimp are lightly pink, then rotate on each side for at least a minute or so – until firm and pink. Remove from heat and serve immediately. 370 calories per serving. Serves 6.

Protein 48   Carbohydrate 5.1   Fat 16.3   Cholesterol 443

Creamy Corn Pudding

❧

½	cup sugar
3	tablespoons corn starch
2	eggs, beaten
16	ounces cream style corn
14	ounces evaporated milk
3	tablespoons butter

Heat oven to 350 degrees. Grease a 1½ quart baking dish. In a bowl, combine sugar and corn starch; add eggs, corn, and milk. Pour into baking dish, and dot with butter. Bake 60 minutes until center is firm. 308 calories per serving. Serves 6.

Protein 8.3   Carbohydrate 42   Fat 12.3   Cholesterol 123

Lima Bean Casserole

❧

This is an economical recipe I started using while we were still in college. Serve with a lettuce wedge and Thousand Island dressing and cornbread.

16	ounces small lima beans
2	beef bouillon cubes
½	cup warm water
½	teaspoon salt
½	teaspoon onion powder
½	teaspoon celery seeds
½	teaspoon sugar
2	tablespoons diced bell pepper
¼	teaspoon garlic powder
¼	cup diced celery
	Cumin and oregano to taste
1	cup grated low fat Cheddar cheese

Rinse beans, pick over, and place in bowl. Cover beans with boiling water, cover bowl, and soak at least 2 hours. Drain beans and place in a medium size pot. Dissolve bouillon cubes in water and add along with remaining ingredients, except the cheese, to the soup pot. Cover with water. Simmer for 1½ hours. Place in a casserole dish; add water to cover. Top with shredded cheese. Cover and place in a 350 oven for 20 to 30 minutes. 253 calories per serving. Serves 6.

Protein 19.5   Carbohydrate 40.4   Fat 2.1   Cholesterol 6.7

Rhonda Walters with daughter, Elizabeth, on the second floor balcony overlooking the South Lawn.

Doris Cross' Old Fashioned Chicken and Dumplings

One of Governor Walters' favorites!

4   chicken breasts, boneless, skinless, and cut in chunks
28   ounces chicken broth
3   cups water
1   medium onion, chopped
¼   teaspoon garlic powder
½   cup finely chopped celery
¼   teaspoon poultry seasoning
1   teaspoon parsley
     Salt and pepper to taste

Add chicken to a large pot coated with a non-stick cooking spray. Brown chicken before adding broth, water, and remaining ingredients. Simmer uncovered for 30 minutes over low heat.

Dumplings

3   egg whites
½   cup low fat cottage cheese
⅛   cup water
     Pinch of salt
1   cup flour

To prepare dumplings, beat egg whites and cottage cheese with electric mixer. Add water and salt, and mix till well blended. Add one half cup flour and combine thoroughly, by hand. Gradually stir in remaining flour. Blend well.

To cook dumplings, drop a tablespoon of dough at a time into boiling chicken stock. After all the dumplings have been added to broth, turn down the heat, cover, and cook for 15 minutes. If a thicker, richer broth is preferred, uncover and cook a few minutes longer. 167 calories per serving. Serves approximately 6 to 8.

Protein 20.5   Carbohydrate 13.6   Fat 2.9   Cholesterol 37.6

Casual Chicken Kiev

*For a more elegant dinner,
use boneless whole chicken breasts.*

1	cup Land of Lakes Sweet Cream Spread
⅔	cup fine dry bread crumbs
3	tablespoons fresh Parmesan cheese, grated
1	teaspoon chopped fresh basil leaves
1	teaspoon chopped fresh oregano leaves
⅔	teaspoon finely chopped garlic
	Salt to taste
3	chicken breasts, split and skinless
⅓	cup dry white wine
½	cup chopped green onion
¼	cup finely chopped parsley
3	cups cooked rice

Preheat oven to 375 degrees. In a heavy 2 quart saucepan, melt cream spread. In a large bowl, combine bread crumbs, Parmesan cheese, basil, oregano, garlic, and salt. Dip chicken breasts in cream spread, then coat with crumb mixture.

Place in ungreased 9 inch square baking dish and bake in center of oven for 50 to 60 minutes, until chicken is golden brown and tender. Meanwhile, add wine, green onion, and parsley to remaining cream spread. Pour over the baked chicken.

Return to oven for approximately 5 minutes until sauce is hot. Serve with cooked rice. 704 calories per serving. Serves 6.

Protein 37   Carbohydrate 38.4   Fat 43.4   Cholesterol 177

Oven Meatballs with Sauerbraten Sauce

2	pounds ground beef
1½	cups soft bread crumbs (3 bread slices)
½	cup milk
¼	cup onion, finely chopped
1	egg
1½	teaspoons salt

Preheat oven to 375 degrees. Combine all ingredients and thoroughly mix. Shape into meatballs and place in 15½ by 10½ by 1 inch baking dish. Bake 25 to 30 minutes.

Sauerbraten Sauce

3	cups water
4	beef bouillon cubes
12	tablespoons brown sugar
8	tablespoons raisins
8	tablespoons lemon juice
1	cup coarse gingersnap crumbs
	Hot cooked rice

Combine first 5 ingredients and heat to boiling. Add gingersnap crumbs and stir until thickened. Add meatballs to sauce. Serve over rice. 519 calories per serving. Serves 8.

Protein 33.7   Carbohydrate 49   Fat 21.3   Cholesterol 131

Curried Orange Chicken

3	pound fryer, cut up, or chicken breasts and/or thighs
1½	teaspoons curry powder
1	cup freshly squeezed orange juice
8	tablespoons honey
4	tablespoons prepared mustard
	Hot cooked rice

Preheat oven to 375 degrees. Sprinkle and rub chicken with curry powder. Arrange chicken in baking dish, skin side down. Combine orange juice, honey, and mustard in small saucepan, simmer till blended. Pour over chicken and bake uncovered for 30 minutes. Turn chicken and continue baking 20 minutes longer or until tender. Serve over rice. 460 calories per serving. Serves 6.

Protein 45.5   Carbohydrate 28   Fat 17.8   Cholesterol 141

Cream Cheese Brownie Cake

*From Doris Cross'
"Fat Free and Ultra Low Fat Recipes"*

1½	cups flour
1	cup sugar
½	teaspoon baking soda
¼	cup dry cocoa
⅛	teaspoon salt
1	cup water
½	teaspoon vinegar
1	teaspoon vanilla
¼	cup fat free mayonnaise
⅛	cup light corn syrup

Preheat oven to 350 degrees. In a large bowl, combine flour, sugar, soda, cocoa, and salt. Stir until well blended. Add water, vinegar, vanilla, mayonnaise, and corn syrup. Mix with electric blender until smooth. Spray 9 inch baking pan with a non-stick cooking spray and add batter. Set aside while making the Cream Cheese Swirl.

Cream Cheese Swirl

⅓	cup lite cream cheese
1½	tablespoons sugar
¼	teaspoon vanilla

In a bowl, mix the cream cheese, sugar, and vanilla with blender until smooth and creamy. Drop 1 tablespoon of this mixture in four or five different places on top of the batter.

Insert a table knife in the center of each cream cheese drop and swirl the mixture through the batter. Curve the knife to make pretty swirls on top of the batter. Bake 40-50 minutes. 380 calories per serving. Serves 6 to 8.

Protein 5.4   Carbohydrate 66   Fat 11.6   Cholesterol 17.8

Streusel Pecan Pie Squares

Great for entertaining a crowd.

Crust

3	cups all purpose flour
¾	cup packed brown sugar
1½	cups margarine, chilled

Filling

¾	cup packed brown sugar
1½	cups corn syrup
1	cup milk
⅓	cup margarine, melted
1	teaspoon vanilla
4	eggs
1½	cups chopped pecans

Preheat oven to 400 degrees. Combine all crust ingredients in a large mixing bowl and blend until crumbly. Reserve 2 cups of crust for filling and topping. Using an ungreased 15 by 10 inch jelly roll pan, press crust in bottom and ¾ inch up the sides of the pan. Bake for 10 minutes.

Mix one-fourth cup of the reserved crumbs with the filling ingredients, except pecans, and blend well. Add pecans. Pour over prebaked crust; return to oven and bake 10 minutes.

Sprinkle remaining 1¾ cups crumbs over filling. Bake at 350 degrees until crumbs are golden, for 20 to 25 minutes. 545 calories per serving. Serves 15.

Protein 5.4   Carbohydrate 63   Fat 31.5   Cholesterol 74

Mousse au Chocolat

This recipe, a dessert at the wonderful Cellar Restaurant in Oklahoma City's Hightower Building, was served frequently in the Mansion by Ann Bartlett Burke, wife of former Governor Dewey Bartlett.

15   ounces sweet German chocolate
¼   pound unsalted butter
⅜   cup white corn syrup
1   cup sugar
¼   cup water
½   cup egg yolks
1   cup egg whites
1½   cups whipping cream, stiffly whipped
      Chopped pistachio nuts

Melt the chocolate and butter in a double boiler. Cook corn syrup, sugar, and water until mixture spins an 8 inch thread and yields ½ cup. Beat the yolks until thick, slowly add syrup to yolks. Add cooled, melted chocolate to this mixture.

Beat egg whites to stiff peaks; fold into chocolate. Place in stainless steel bowl and set two hours in refrigerator. Remove from refrigerator. To bowl of chocolate, add 1 cup cream and beat until fluffy rich chocolate. Decorate with the remaining whipped cream and garnish with chopped pistachio nuts. 728 calories per serving. Serves 8.

Protein 9.4   Carbohydrate 63   Fat 55   Cholesterol 267

The second floor balcony overlooking the Mansion's South Lawn.

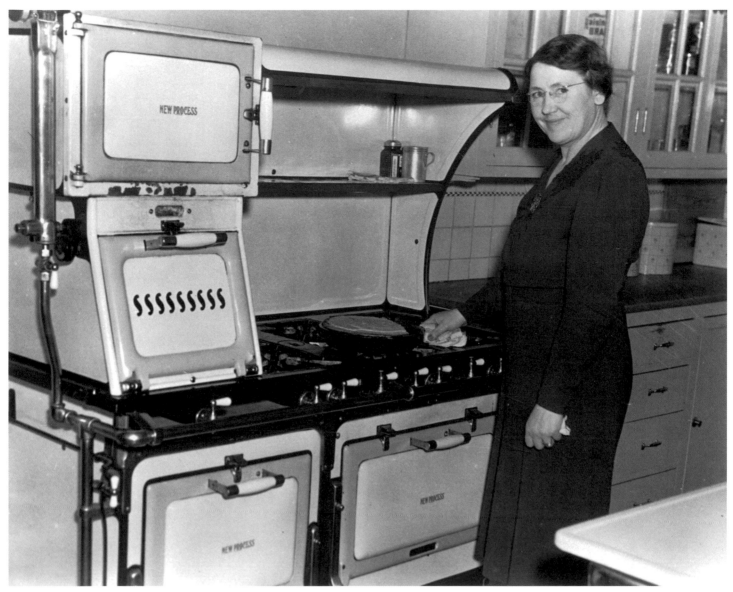

Mrs. Leon C. Phillips in the Mansion kitchen. Her husband was governor from 1939 to 1943.

acknowledgements

The following people have been of tremendous help in compiling this book.

Jeffrey Briley, curator of the State Museum of History.
Photographs courtesy of the Archives Division, Oklahoma
Historical Society, appear on pages 8, 9, 10, 11, 21, 69, and 109.
Historical Artifacts courtesy of Oklahoma Historical Society.

Oklahoma Health Department for nutritional analyses.

Ann Whittaker, owner of "Once Upon a Tabletop" for tablecloths,
dishes, and decorations.

Norma Townsend, Alicia McCoy, and Sally Mahaffey for
table decorations.

J.B. Pratt of Pratt's Foods.

Linda Trippe and Frannie Pasternik of
Trippe Catering.

Bill Gooch, Photographer, page 5.

Steven F. Bunch, Oklahoma Governor's Mansion Administrator.

Sharen Lenhart,
Administrative Assistant
to First Lady Rhonda Walters.

index